50 Sugar-Free Treat Recipes for Home

By: Kelly Johnson

Table of Contents

- Sugar-Free Chocolate Avocado Mousse
- Keto Peanut Butter Cookies
- Stevia-Sweetened Lemon Bars
- No-Bake Sugar-Free Cheesecake Bites
- Almond Flour Brownies
- Coconut Macaroons (Sweetened with Erythritol)
- Sugar-Free Vanilla Chia Pudding
- Low-Carb Raspberry Cheesecake Bars
- Avocado Chocolate Pudding
- Sugar-Free Pumpkin Spice Muffins
- Almond Butter Fat Bombs
- Flourless Sugar-Free Chocolate Cake
- Keto Lemon Poppy Seed Muffins
- Coconut Flour Pancakes
- Chocolate-Dipped Strawberries (Sweetened with Stevia)
- No-Bake Almond Butter Energy Balls
- Sugar-Free Blueberry Cheesecake
- Cinnamon Walnut Keto Granola
- Zucchini Chocolate Chip Cookies
- Creamy Sugar-Free Popsicles (Various Flavors)
- Keto Chocolate Chip Cookie Dough Fat Bombs
- Peanut Butter Chocolate Chip Mug Cake
- Sugar-Free Coconut Cream Pie
- Lemon Coconut Energy Balls
- Low-Carb Chocolate Avocado Truffles
- Almond Flour Shortbread Cookies
- Sugar-Free Raspberry Coconut Squares
- Pumpkin Spice Energy Bites
- Keto Chocolate Peanut Butter Cups
- No-Bake Sugar-Free Key Lime Pie
- Blueberry Almond Scones
- Sugar-Free Greek Yogurt Parfait
- Chocolate Hazelnut Fat Bombs
- Vanilla Almond Flour Cake
- Keto Pecan Pie Bars

- Sugar-Free Apple Cinnamon Muffins
- Avocado Lime Cheesecake Bites
- Almond Butter Chocolate Fudge
- Raspberry Almond Flour Blondies
- Sugar-Free Matcha Chia Pudding
- No-Bake Coconut Lime Energy Bites
- Keto Chocolate Mint Cookies
- Peanut Butter Banana Smoothie (Sweetened with Stevia)
- Sugar-Free Lemon Coconut Macaroons
- Almond Flour Zucchini Bread
- Chocolate Almond Butter Cups
- Low-Carb Pumpkin Cheesecake Bars
- Sugar-Free Cinnamon Apple Crisp
- Blueberry Coconut Flour Muffins
- Avocado Lime Ice Cream

Sugar-Free Chocolate Avocado Mousse

Ingredients:

- 2 ripe avocados
- 1/3 cup unsweetened cocoa powder
- 1/3 cup milk (almond milk or coconut milk for dairy-free)
- 1/4 cup sugar-free sweetener (erythritol, stevia, or monk fruit sweetener)
- 1 tsp vanilla extract
- Pinch of salt
- Optional toppings: whipped cream (sugar-free), berries, chopped nuts

Instructions:

1. **Prepare the Avocados**: Cut the avocados in half, remove the pit, and scoop out the flesh into a food processor or blender.
2. **Blend**: Add cocoa powder, milk, sugar-free sweetener, vanilla extract, and a pinch of salt to the blender or food processor.
3. **Blend Until Smooth**: Blend until the mixture is smooth and creamy, scraping down the sides of the blender or food processor as needed.
4. **Adjust Sweetness**: Taste and adjust sweetness as needed. Add more sweetener if desired.
5. **Chill**: Transfer the mousse to serving dishes or a large bowl, cover, and refrigerate for at least 30 minutes to chill and firm up.
6. **Serve**: Serve chilled, optionally topped with sugar-free whipped cream, berries, or chopped nuts.
7. **Enjoy**: Enjoy your guilt-free, creamy chocolate avocado mousse!

This dessert is rich in healthy fats from avocados and provides a satisfying chocolate flavor without the added sugar, making it a great option for those looking to reduce their sugar intake while still enjoying a delicious treat.

Keto Peanut Butter Cookies

Ingredients:

- 1 cup natural peanut butter (unsweetened, creamy or crunchy)
- 1/2 cup sugar-free sweetener (erythritol or monk fruit sweetener)
- 1 large egg
- 1 teaspoon vanilla extract
- 1/2 teaspoon baking soda
- Pinch of salt

Instructions:

1. **Preheat Oven**: Preheat your oven to 350°F (175°C). Line a baking sheet with parchment paper or a silicone baking mat.
2. **Mix Ingredients**: In a mixing bowl, combine the peanut butter, sugar-free sweetener, egg, vanilla extract, baking soda, and a pinch of salt. Mix until well combined and smooth.
3. **Form Cookies**: Scoop out tablespoon-sized portions of the dough and roll them into balls. Place them on the prepared baking sheet, leaving space between each cookie.
4. **Flatten Cookies**: Use a fork to flatten each cookie slightly, creating a crisscross pattern.
5. **Bake**: Bake the cookies in the preheated oven for 10-12 minutes, or until the edges are lightly golden.
6. **Cool**: Allow the cookies to cool on the baking sheet for a few minutes before transferring them to a wire rack to cool completely.
7. **Enjoy**: Once cooled, enjoy your delicious Keto Peanut Butter Cookies! Store any leftovers in an airtight container at room temperature.

These cookies are low-carb and keto-friendly, perfect for anyone looking for a sugar-free treat that still satisfies the peanut butter cookie cravings!

Stevia-Sweetened Lemon Bars

Ingredients:

For the Crust:

- 1 cup almond flour
- 1/4 cup coconut flour
- 1/4 cup melted coconut oil
- 1/4 cup powdered stevia or stevia blend
- Pinch of salt

For the Lemon Filling:

- 4 large eggs
- 3/4 cup fresh lemon juice (about 4-5 lemons)
- Zest of 2 lemons
- 1/2 cup powdered stevia or stevia blend
- 1/4 cup almond flour
- 1/4 cup coconut flour
- 1/4 cup melted coconut oil
- 1/2 teaspoon baking powder
- Powdered stevia, for dusting (optional)

Instructions:

1. **Preheat Oven and Prepare Pan**: Preheat your oven to 350°F (175°C). Line an 8x8 inch baking pan with parchment paper, leaving some overhang for easy removal.
2. **Make the Crust**:
    - In a mixing bowl, combine almond flour, coconut flour, melted coconut oil, powdered stevia, and a pinch of salt.
    - Mix until well combined and press the mixture evenly into the bottom of the prepared baking pan.
3. **Bake the Crust**: Bake the crust in the preheated oven for 10-12 minutes, or until lightly golden. Remove from oven and set aside.
4. **Prepare the Lemon Filling**:
    - In another mixing bowl, whisk together eggs, fresh lemon juice, lemon zest, and powdered stevia until smooth.
    - Add almond flour, coconut flour, melted coconut oil, and baking powder. Mix until well combined and smooth.

5. **Assemble and Bake**:
   - Pour the lemon filling over the pre-baked crust, spreading it out evenly.
   - Return the pan to the oven and bake for 20-25 minutes, or until the filling is set and the edges are lightly golden.
6. **Cool and Chill**:
   - Remove the pan from the oven and let the lemon bars cool completely in the pan on a wire rack.
   - Once cooled, transfer the pan to the refrigerator and chill for at least 2 hours to firm up.
7. **Serve**:
   - Once chilled, lift the lemon bars out of the pan using the parchment paper overhang. Cut into squares.
   - Dust with powdered stevia, if desired, before serving.
8. **Enjoy**:
   - Serve and enjoy these refreshing Stevia-Sweetened Lemon Bars as a sugar-free treat!

These lemon bars are tangy, sweetened with stevia instead of sugar, and have a delicious almond and coconut flour crust that complements the citrusy lemon filling perfectly.

No-Bake Sugar-Free Cheesecake Bites

Ingredients:

For the Crust:

- 1 cup almond flour
- 3 tablespoons melted coconut oil
- 1 tablespoon powdered stevia or stevia blend
- Pinch of salt

For the Cheesecake Filling:

- 8 ounces cream cheese, softened
- 1/4 cup powdered stevia or stevia blend (adjust to taste)
- 1 teaspoon vanilla extract
- Juice of half a lemon
- 1/4 cup heavy cream (or coconut cream for dairy-free option)

Optional Topping:

- Sugar-free chocolate chips, berries, or a sprinkle of cocoa powder for decoration

Instructions:

1. **Prepare the Crust:**
    - In a mixing bowl, combine almond flour, melted coconut oil, powdered stevia, and a pinch of salt.
    - Mix until well combined and the mixture resembles coarse crumbs.
2. **Form Crust Base:**
    - Line a mini muffin tin with mini muffin liners.
    - Spoon about 1 tablespoon of the crust mixture into each liner.
    - Press the mixture firmly into the bottom of each liner to form a crust layer.
3. **Make the Cheesecake Filling:**
    - In a separate mixing bowl, beat the softened cream cheese until smooth and creamy.
    - Add powdered stevia, vanilla extract, lemon juice, and heavy cream (or coconut cream).
    - Beat until well combined and smooth.
4. **Fill the Muffin Liners:**

- Spoon or pipe the cheesecake filling evenly into each muffin liner over the crust layer.
5. **Chill:**
    - Place the muffin tin in the refrigerator and chill for at least 2 hours, or until the cheesecake bites are firm.
6. **Optional Decoration:**
    - Before serving, you can optionally top each cheesecake bite with sugar-free chocolate chips, berries, or a sprinkle of cocoa powder.
7. **Serve and Enjoy:**
    - Remove the cheesecake bites from the muffin tin and peel off the liners.
    - Arrange on a serving plate and serve chilled.

These No-Bake Sugar-Free Cheesecake Bites are creamy, satisfying, and perfect for a guilt-free dessert or snack option. They're easy to make and can be customized with various toppings to suit your taste preferences!

Almond Flour Brownies

Ingredients:

- 1/2 cup (1 stick) unsalted butter, melted
- 1/2 cup powdered stevia or stevia blend (adjust to taste)
- 2 large eggs
- 1 teaspoon vanilla extract
- 1/2 cup unsweetened cocoa powder
- 1/2 cup almond flour
- 1/2 teaspoon baking powder
- 1/4 teaspoon salt
- 1/2 cup sugar-free chocolate chips (optional)

Instructions:

1. **Preheat Oven**: Preheat your oven to 350°F (175°C). Grease or line an 8x8 inch baking pan with parchment paper.
2. **Mix Wet Ingredients**: In a mixing bowl, combine melted butter and powdered stevia. Mix until well combined.
3. **Add Eggs and Vanilla**: Add the eggs and vanilla extract to the butter mixture. Beat until smooth.
4. **Combine Dry Ingredients**: In another bowl, whisk together cocoa powder, almond flour, baking powder, and salt.
5. **Mix Batter**: Gradually add the dry ingredients to the wet ingredients, stirring until just combined. Do not overmix.
6. **Optional: Add Chocolate Chips**: Fold in sugar-free chocolate chips if desired, reserving some for topping.
7. **Bake**: Pour the batter into the prepared baking pan, spreading it out evenly. If desired, sprinkle additional chocolate chips on top.
8. **Bake**: Bake in the preheated oven for 20-25 minutes, or until a toothpick inserted into the center comes out with a few moist crumbs.
9. **Cool**: Allow the brownies to cool completely in the pan on a wire rack.
10. **Slice and Serve**: Once cooled, slice into squares and serve. Enjoy your delicious sugar-free Almond Flour Brownies!

These brownies are rich, chocolaty, and have a fudgy texture thanks to the almond flour. They're perfect for satisfying your chocolate cravings without the guilt of added sugar.

Coconut Macaroons (Sweetened with Erythritol)

Ingredients:

- 3 cups unsweetened shredded coconut
- 3/4 cup powdered erythritol (or another sugar-free sweetener of your choice)
- 1/3 cup coconut flour
- 1/4 teaspoon salt
- 3 large egg whites
- 1 teaspoon vanilla extract
- 1/4 cup melted coconut oil

Instructions:

1. **Preheat Oven**: Preheat your oven to 325°F (160°C). Line a baking sheet with parchment paper.
2. **Mix Dry Ingredients**: In a large bowl, combine the shredded coconut, powdered erythritol, coconut flour, and salt. Mix well.
3. **Whip Egg Whites**: In a separate bowl, whip the egg whites with a hand mixer or stand mixer until stiff peaks form.
4. **Combine Ingredients**: Gently fold the whipped egg whites into the coconut mixture until well combined. Add vanilla extract and melted coconut oil, and mix until everything is evenly incorporated.
5. **Form Macaroons**: Using a spoon or cookie scoop, scoop out about 1-2 tablespoons of the mixture and shape it into a compact mound using your hands. Place each macaroon onto the prepared baking sheet, leaving a little space between each one.
6. **Bake**: Bake in the preheated oven for 20-25 minutes, or until the macaroons are lightly golden on the edges and firm to the touch.
7. **Cool**: Allow the macaroons to cool completely on the baking sheet before transferring them to a wire rack.
8. **Enjoy**: Once cooled, enjoy your sugar-free Coconut Macaroons! Store any leftovers in an airtight container at room temperature.

These coconut macaroons are chewy on the inside and lightly crisp on the outside, with a delicious coconut flavor that's perfectly complemented by the erythritol sweetness. They're a wonderful treat for anyone looking to indulge in a sugar-free dessert option.

Sugar-Free Vanilla Chia Pudding

Ingredients:

- 1/4 cup chia seeds
- 1 cup unsweetened almond milk (or any milk of your choice)
- 1-2 tablespoons powdered erythritol (or sweetener of your choice), adjust to taste
- 1 teaspoon vanilla extract
- Optional toppings: fresh berries, nuts, coconut flakes

Instructions:

1. **Mix Ingredients**: In a bowl or jar, combine chia seeds, unsweetened almond milk, powdered erythritol (or sweetener of choice), and vanilla extract. Stir well to combine.
2. **Sweeten to Taste**: Taste the mixture and adjust sweetness if needed by adding more powdered erythritol.
3. **Set Aside and Stir**: Let the mixture sit for about 5 minutes, then stir again to break up any clumps of chia seeds.
4. **Chill**: Cover the bowl or jar and refrigerate for at least 2 hours, or overnight. The chia seeds will absorb the liquid and thicken to form a pudding-like consistency.
5. **Serve**: Once chilled and thickened, stir the chia pudding again to distribute evenly. Serve in individual bowls or jars.
6. **Add Toppings**: Optionally, top with fresh berries, nuts, or coconut flakes for added texture and flavor.
7. **Enjoy**: Enjoy your creamy and sugar-free Vanilla Chia Pudding as a healthy breakfast, snack, or dessert option!

This pudding is not only delicious but also packed with fiber and omega-3 fatty acids from the chia seeds, making it a nutritious choice for those looking to cut down on sugar without sacrificing flavor. Adjust the sweetness and toppings according to your preferences for a personalized treat.

Low-Carb Raspberry Cheesecake Bars

Ingredients:

For the Crust:

- 1 cup almond flour
- 1/4 cup powdered erythritol (or another sugar-free sweetener)
- 1/4 cup melted butter

For the Cheesecake Filling:

- 16 ounces cream cheese, softened
- 1/2 cup powdered erythritol (adjust to taste)
- 2 large eggs
- 1 teaspoon vanilla extract
- 1/2 cup fresh or frozen raspberries (thawed if using frozen)

For Raspberry Swirl (optional):

- 1/4 cup fresh or frozen raspberries
- 1 tablespoon powdered erythritol

Instructions:

1. **Preheat Oven**: Preheat your oven to 325°F (160°C). Line an 8x8 inch baking pan with parchment paper, leaving some overhang for easy removal.
2. **Make the Crust**:
   - In a mixing bowl, combine almond flour, powdered erythritol, and melted butter. Mix until well combined and crumbly.
   - Press the mixture evenly into the bottom of the prepared baking pan to form the crust layer.
3. **Prepare the Cheesecake Filling**:
   - In a separate mixing bowl, beat the softened cream cheese and powdered erythritol until smooth and creamy.
   - Add eggs, one at a time, beating well after each addition.
   - Stir in vanilla extract until combined.
4. **Assemble the Bars**:
   - Pour the cheesecake filling over the prepared crust in the baking pan, spreading it out evenly with a spatula.
5. **Optional Raspberry Swirl**:

- If using the raspberry swirl, blend or mash raspberries with powdered erythritol until smooth.
- Drop spoonfuls of the raspberry mixture onto the cheesecake layer. Use a toothpick or knife to swirl it into the cheesecake filling for a marbled effect.

6. **Bake**:
   - Bake in the preheated oven for 30-35 minutes, or until the edges are set and the center is slightly jiggly.
7. **Cool and Chill**:
   - Remove from the oven and let the cheesecake bars cool completely in the pan on a wire rack.
   - Once cooled, refrigerate for at least 2 hours, or overnight, to firm up.
8. **Slice and Serve**:
   - Lift the cheesecake bars out of the pan using the parchment paper overhang. Cut into squares.
9. **Enjoy**:
   - Serve chilled, optionally garnished with fresh raspberries or a dusting of powdered erythritol.

These Low-Carb Raspberry Cheesecake Bars are creamy, tangy, and bursting with raspberry flavor, making them a perfect guilt-free treat for those on a low-carb or keto diet. Adjust the sweetness and tartness to your liking by varying the amount of sweetener and raspberry swirl.

Avocado Chocolate Pudding

Ingredients:

- 2 ripe avocados
- 1/2 cup unsweetened cocoa powder
- 1/2 cup almond milk (or any milk of your choice)
- 1/4 cup powdered erythritol (or sweetener of your choice), adjust to taste
- 2 teaspoons vanilla extract
- Pinch of salt
- Optional toppings: whipped coconut cream, berries, shaved chocolate

Instructions:

1. **Prepare the Avocados**: Cut the avocados in half, remove the pit, and scoop out the flesh into a food processor or blender.
2. **Blend**: Add cocoa powder, almond milk, powdered erythritol, vanilla extract, and a pinch of salt to the blender or food processor.
3. **Blend Until Smooth**: Blend until the mixture is smooth and creamy, scraping down the sides of the blender or food processor as needed.
4. **Adjust Sweetness**: Taste and adjust sweetness as needed by adding more powdered erythritol.
5. **Chill**: Transfer the pudding to serving dishes or a large bowl, cover, and refrigerate for at least 30 minutes to chill and allow the flavors to meld.
6. **Serve**: Serve chilled, optionally topped with whipped coconut cream, berries, or shaved chocolate.
7. **Enjoy**: Enjoy your creamy and indulgent Avocado Chocolate Pudding! It's a perfect guilt-free dessert or snack option.

This pudding is rich in healthy fats from avocados and antioxidants from cocoa powder, making it not only delicious but also nutritious. It's a great way to satisfy your chocolate cravings while enjoying a dessert that's sugar-free and dairy-free. Adjust the sweetness and texture to your preference for the perfect avocado chocolate pudding experience!

Sugar-Free Pumpkin Spice Muffins

Ingredients:

- 1 cup almond flour
- 1/4 cup coconut flour
- 1/4 cup powdered erythritol (or sweetener of your choice)
- 1 teaspoon baking powder
- 1/2 teaspoon baking soda
- 1/2 teaspoon salt
- 1 teaspoon ground cinnamon
- 1/2 teaspoon ground ginger
- 1/4 teaspoon ground nutmeg
- 1/4 teaspoon ground cloves
- 1/2 cup pumpkin puree
- 1/4 cup melted coconut oil
- 3 large eggs
- 1 teaspoon vanilla extract

Instructions:

1. **Preheat Oven**: Preheat your oven to 350°F (175°C). Line a muffin tin with paper liners or grease well.
2. **Mix Dry Ingredients**: In a large bowl, whisk together almond flour, coconut flour, powdered erythritol, baking powder, baking soda, salt, cinnamon, ginger, nutmeg, and cloves until well combined.
3. **Mix Wet Ingredients**: In another bowl, whisk together pumpkin puree, melted coconut oil, eggs, and vanilla extract until smooth.
4. **Combine Wet and Dry Ingredients**: Pour the wet ingredients into the bowl of dry ingredients. Stir until just combined, being careful not to overmix.
5. **Fill Muffin Cups**: Divide the batter evenly among the muffin cups, filling each about 3/4 full.
6. **Bake**: Bake in the preheated oven for 20-25 minutes, or until a toothpick inserted into the center comes out clean.
7. **Cool**: Remove the muffin tin from the oven and let the muffins cool in the tin for 5 minutes. Then transfer them to a wire rack to cool completely.
8. **Serve**: Enjoy your Sugar-Free Pumpkin Spice Muffins warm or at room temperature.

These muffins are moist, flavorful, and perfect for enjoying the warm spices of fall without the added sugar. They make a great breakfast, snack, or dessert option that's low-carb and keto-friendly. Adjust the sweetness and spice levels to suit your taste preferences for the perfect sugar-free treat!

Almond Butter Fat Bombs

Ingredients:

- 1/2 cup almond butter (unsweetened)
- 1/4 cup coconut oil, melted
- 2 tablespoons powdered erythritol (or sweetener of your choice), adjust to taste
- 1/2 teaspoon vanilla extract
- Pinch of salt
- Optional: 2-3 tablespoons chopped almonds or dark chocolate chips for coating

Instructions:

1. **Mix Ingredients**: In a bowl, combine almond butter, melted coconut oil, powdered erythritol, vanilla extract, and a pinch of salt. Mix until smooth and well combined.
2. **Form Fat Bombs**: Scoop the mixture into silicone molds or shape them into balls using your hands. If desired, press a few chopped almonds or dark chocolate chips onto each fat bomb.
3. **Chill**: Place the fat bombs in the refrigerator or freezer to set for at least 30 minutes, until firm.
4. **Optional Coating**: If you prefer, melt some dark chocolate and dip each fat bomb to coat. Place them back in the refrigerator to allow the chocolate to harden.
5. **Store**: Keep the almond butter fat bombs stored in an airtight container in the refrigerator or freezer.
6. **Enjoy**: Grab one whenever you need a quick and satisfying snack!

These almond butter fat bombs are high in healthy fats, low in carbs, and provide a boost of energy, making them ideal for maintaining ketosis or as a convenient snack on the go. Adjust the sweetness and add-ins to suit your taste preferences.

Flourless Sugar-Free Chocolate Cake

Ingredients:

- 1 cup sugar-free chocolate chips (make sure they are keto-friendly)
- 1/2 cup unsalted butter
- 3/4 cup powdered erythritol (or sweetener of your choice)
- 1/4 teaspoon salt
- 1 teaspoon vanilla extract
- 3 large eggs
- 1/2 cup unsweetened cocoa powder

Instructions:

1. **Preheat Oven**: Preheat your oven to 350°F (175°C). Grease a 9-inch round cake pan and line the bottom with parchment paper.
2. **Melt Chocolate and Butter**: In a microwave-safe bowl or using a double boiler, melt the chocolate chips and butter together until smooth. Stir occasionally to combine.
3. **Mix Sweetener and Salt**: Stir in powdered erythritol (or sweetener of your choice), salt, and vanilla extract into the melted chocolate mixture.
4. **Add Eggs**: Add eggs, one at a time, mixing well after each addition.
5. **Add Cocoa Powder**: Sift in cocoa powder and mix until smooth and well combined.
6. **Bake**: Pour the batter into the prepared cake pan and smooth the top with a spatula.
7. **Bake**: Bake in the preheated oven for 25-30 minutes, or until the cake is set and a toothpick inserted into the center comes out with a few moist crumbs.
8. **Cool**: Allow the cake to cool in the pan for about 10 minutes, then carefully invert onto a wire rack to cool completely.
9. **Serve**: Slice and serve your flourless sugar-free chocolate cake. Optionally, dust with powdered erythritol or cocoa powder before serving.

This cake is dense, moist, and intensely chocolatey, making it a perfect treat for those on a keto or low-carb diet. It's also gluten-free due to the absence of flour. Enjoy it with a dollop of whipped cream or a scoop of sugar-free ice cream for an extra indulgent dessert!

Keto Lemon Poppy Seed Muffins

Ingredients:

- 2 cups almond flour
- 1/3 cup powdered erythritol (or sweetener of your choice)
- 1 tablespoon poppy seeds
- 1 tablespoon lemon zest (from about 2 lemons)
- 1 teaspoon baking powder
- 1/4 teaspoon salt
- 1/3 cup melted coconut oil
- 1/4 cup fresh lemon juice (from about 2 lemons)
- 3 large eggs
- 1 teaspoon vanilla extract

Instructions:

1. **Preheat Oven**: Preheat your oven to 350°F (175°C). Line a muffin tin with paper liners or grease well.
2. **Mix Dry Ingredients**: In a large bowl, whisk together almond flour, powdered erythritol, poppy seeds, lemon zest, baking powder, and salt until well combined.
3. **Mix Wet Ingredients**: In another bowl, whisk together melted coconut oil, lemon juice, eggs, and vanilla extract until smooth.
4. **Combine**: Pour the wet ingredients into the bowl of dry ingredients. Stir until just combined, being careful not to overmix.
5. **Fill Muffin Cups**: Divide the batter evenly among the muffin cups, filling each about 3/4 full.
6. **Bake**: Bake in the preheated oven for 20-25 minutes, or until a toothpick inserted into the center comes out clean.
7. **Cool**: Remove the muffin tin from the oven and let the muffins cool in the tin for 5 minutes. Then transfer them to a wire rack to cool completely.
8. **Serve**: Enjoy your Keto Lemon Poppy Seed Muffins warm or at room temperature.

These muffins are moist, flavorful, and have a lovely citrusy kick from the lemon zest and juice. They make a great breakfast or snack option for those on a keto or low-carb diet. Adjust the sweetness and lemon flavor to suit your taste preferences for the perfect keto treat!

Coconut Flour Pancakes

Ingredients:

- 1/4 cup coconut flour
- 1 tablespoon powdered erythritol (or sweetener of your choice)
- 1/2 teaspoon baking powder
- Pinch of salt
- 3 large eggs
- 1/4 cup unsweetened almond milk (or any milk of your choice)
- 1 teaspoon vanilla extract
- Butter or coconut oil, for cooking

Instructions:

1. **Mix Dry Ingredients**: In a bowl, whisk together coconut flour, powdered erythritol, baking powder, and a pinch of salt until well combined and no lumps remain.
2. **Mix Wet Ingredients**: In another bowl, whisk together eggs, almond milk, and vanilla extract until smooth.
3. **Combine**: Pour the wet ingredients into the bowl of dry ingredients. Stir until well combined and smooth. Let the batter sit for a few minutes to allow the coconut flour to absorb the liquid (the batter will thicken slightly).
4. **Cook Pancakes**: Heat a non-stick skillet or griddle over medium heat. Add a small amount of butter or coconut oil to coat the surface.
5. **Spoon Batter**: Spoon about 2 tablespoons of batter onto the skillet for each pancake, spreading it slightly with the back of the spoon to form circles.
6. **Cook Until Bubbles**: Cook for 2-3 minutes, or until bubbles start to form on the surface of the pancake and the edges begin to set.
7. **Flip and Cook**: Carefully flip the pancakes with a spatula and cook for another 1-2 minutes on the other side, until golden brown and cooked through.
8. **Serve**: Repeat with the remaining batter. Serve the coconut flour pancakes warm with your favorite toppings such as sugar-free syrup, fresh berries, or whipped cream.

These coconut flour pancakes are fluffy, flavorful, and perfect for anyone looking to enjoy a low-carb or keto-friendly breakfast option. They're naturally gluten-free and can be customized with different toppings to suit your taste preferences. Adjust the sweetness level by adding more or less sweetener to the batter as desired. Enjoy your delicious pancakes!

Chocolate-Dipped Strawberries (Sweetened with Stevia)

Ingredients:

- Fresh strawberries, washed and dried
- Sugar-free dark chocolate chips or chopped sugar-free dark chocolate
- Powdered stevia or stevia blend, to taste
- Optional: Coconut oil or butter for thinning chocolate

Instructions:

1. **Prepare Strawberries**: Make sure the strawberries are completely dry before dipping to help the chocolate adhere better.
2. **Melt Chocolate**: In a microwave-safe bowl or over a double boiler, melt the sugar-free dark chocolate until smooth. If using chocolate chips, microwave in 30-second intervals, stirring in between, until melted. If the chocolate seems too thick, you can add a small amount of coconut oil or butter to thin it out.
3. **Sweeten Chocolate**: Stir in powdered stevia or stevia blend to taste. Start with a small amount and adjust based on your sweetness preference.
4. **Dip Strawberries**: Holding the strawberries by the stem, dip each one into the melted chocolate, swirling to coat evenly. Shake off any excess chocolate.
5. **Place on Parchment**: Place the chocolate-dipped strawberries on a parchment-lined baking sheet or plate. This will prevent sticking and make cleanup easier.
6. **Chill**: Place the chocolate-dipped strawberries in the refrigerator for about 10-15 minutes, or until the chocolate sets.
7. **Serve**: Once the chocolate is firm, arrange the strawberries on a serving plate and serve immediately.
8. **Enjoy**: Enjoy your delicious chocolate-dipped strawberries sweetened with stevia as a guilt-free dessert or snack!

These chocolate-dipped strawberries are perfect for special occasions or as a healthier treat option. The combination of sweet strawberries and rich, sugar-free chocolate makes for a delightful and satisfying dessert. Adjust the sweetness and thickness of the chocolate according to your taste preferences.

No-Bake Almond Butter Energy Balls

Ingredients:

- 1 cup old-fashioned rolled oats
- 1/2 cup almond butter (or any nut butter of your choice)
- 1/4 cup honey or maple syrup (for sweetness, adjust to taste)
- 1/4 cup ground flaxseed
- 1/4 cup mini chocolate chips (optional)
- 1 teaspoon vanilla extract
- Pinch of salt (optional)

Instructions:

1. **Mix Ingredients**: In a mixing bowl, combine rolled oats, almond butter, honey or maple syrup, ground flaxseed, mini chocolate chips (if using), vanilla extract, and a pinch of salt.
2. **Combine Thoroughly**: Stir all ingredients together until well combined. The mixture should be sticky enough to hold together when rolled into balls. If it's too dry, add a little more almond butter or honey/maple syrup. If it's too wet, add more oats or flaxseed.
3. **Form Balls**: Using a spoon or your hands, scoop out about 1 tablespoon of the mixture and roll it into a ball between your palms. Repeat with the remaining mixture to make about 12-15 energy balls.
4. **Chill**: Place the energy balls on a baking sheet lined with parchment paper. Chill in the refrigerator for at least 30 minutes to firm up.
5. **Store**: Once chilled and firm, transfer the energy balls to an airtight container. Store them in the refrigerator for up to 1 week, or freeze for longer storage.
6. **Enjoy**: Grab a couple of energy balls whenever you need a quick and nutritious snack!

These no-bake almond butter energy balls are packed with fiber, healthy fats, and protein, making them a great option for pre-workout fuel or a mid-afternoon pick-me-up. Feel free to customize the recipe by adding dried fruit, nuts, or seeds according to your preferences.

Sugar-Free Blueberry Cheesecake

Ingredients:

For the Crust:

- 1 1/2 cups almond flour
- 1/4 cup powdered erythritol (or sweetener of your choice)
- 1/4 cup melted butter

For the Cheesecake Filling:

- 16 ounces cream cheese, softened
- 1/2 cup powdered erythritol (adjust to taste)
- 2 large eggs
- 1 teaspoon vanilla extract
- 1/4 cup sour cream (or Greek yogurt)
- 1 cup fresh or frozen blueberries

For the Blueberry Topping:

- 1 cup fresh or frozen blueberries
- 1-2 tablespoons powdered erythritol (adjust to taste)
- 1 tablespoon water
- 1 teaspoon lemon juice (optional)

Instructions:

1. **Preheat Oven**: Preheat your oven to 325°F (160°C). Grease a 9-inch springform pan or line the bottom with parchment paper.
2. **Make the Crust:**
    - In a bowl, combine almond flour, powdered erythritol, and melted butter. Mix until well combined and press the mixture evenly into the bottom of the prepared springform pan.
3. **Prepare the Cheesecake Filling:**
    - In a large mixing bowl, beat the softened cream cheese and powdered erythritol until smooth and creamy.
    - Add eggs one at a time, beating well after each addition.
    - Mix in vanilla extract and sour cream (or Greek yogurt) until smooth.
4. **Add Blueberries:**
    - Gently fold in 1 cup of blueberries into the cheesecake filling mixture.

5. **Pour and Smooth:**
   - Pour the cheesecake filling over the crust in the springform pan, spreading it out evenly with a spatula.
6. **Bake the Cheesecake:**
   - Place the springform pan on a baking sheet (to catch any potential drips) and bake in the preheated oven for 45-50 minutes, or until the edges are set and the center is slightly jiggly.
7. **Cool and Chill:**
   - Turn off the oven and let the cheesecake cool in the oven with the door slightly open for about 1 hour.
   - Remove from the oven and let it cool completely at room temperature. Refrigerate for at least 4 hours or overnight to firm up.
8. **Make the Blueberry Topping:**
   - In a small saucepan, combine 1 cup of blueberries, powdered erythritol (to taste), water, and lemon juice (if using).
   - Cook over medium heat, stirring occasionally, until the blueberries break down and release their juices, and the mixture thickens slightly (about 5-7 minutes).
   - Remove from heat and let it cool. Refrigerate until ready to use.
9. **Serve:**
   - Once chilled and firm, release the cheesecake from the springform pan and transfer to a serving platter.
   - Spoon the cooled blueberry topping over the cheesecake before serving.
10. **Enjoy:**
    - Slice and serve your delicious Sugar-Free Blueberry Cheesecake, garnished with fresh blueberries if desired.

This sugar-free blueberry cheesecake is a creamy and fruity dessert that's perfect for those on a keto or low-carb diet. The combination of tangy cream cheese filling with a sweet blueberry topping makes it a crowd-pleaser for any occasion. Adjust the sweetness to your taste preferences, and enjoy this guilt-free treat!

Cinnamon Walnut Keto Granola

Ingredients:

- 1 1/2 cups chopped walnuts
- 1 cup unsweetened coconut flakes
- 1/2 cup sliced almonds
- 1/4 cup sunflower seeds
- 1/4 cup pumpkin seeds (pepitas)
- 1/4 cup chia seeds
- 1/4 cup flaxseed meal
- 1/3 cup powdered erythritol (or sweetener of your choice)
- 1 teaspoon ground cinnamon
- 1/4 teaspoon salt
- 1/4 cup melted coconut oil
- 1 teaspoon vanilla extract

Instructions:

1. **Preheat Oven**: Preheat your oven to 300°F (150°C). Line a large baking sheet with parchment paper.
2. **Mix Dry Ingredients**: In a large bowl, combine chopped walnuts, coconut flakes, sliced almonds, sunflower seeds, pumpkin seeds, chia seeds, flaxseed meal, powdered erythritol, ground cinnamon, and salt. Mix well to combine.
3. **Add Wet Ingredients**: Drizzle melted coconut oil and vanilla extract over the dry ingredients. Stir until everything is evenly coated.
4. **Spread on Baking Sheet**: Spread the granola mixture evenly on the prepared baking sheet. Press down lightly with a spatula to compact the mixture slightly.
5. **Bake**: Bake in the preheated oven for 25-30 minutes, stirring halfway through, until the granola is golden brown and crisp.
6. **Cool Completely**: Remove from the oven and let the granola cool completely on the baking sheet. It will continue to crisp up as it cools.
7. **Store**: Once cooled, transfer the granola to an airtight container. Store at room temperature for up to 2 weeks or in the refrigerator for longer freshness.
8. **Serve**: Enjoy your Cinnamon Walnut Keto Granola as a topping for yogurt, a crunchy cereal with almond milk, or as a snack on its own.

This keto granola is packed with healthy fats, fiber, and protein, making it a satisfying option for those on a low-carb or ketogenic diet. Adjust the sweetness and add-ins according to your preferences. It's a versatile recipe that can be customized with different nuts, seeds, or spices to suit your taste!

Zucchini Chocolate Chip Cookies

Ingredients:

- 1 cup shredded zucchini (about 1 medium zucchini)
- 1/4 cup melted coconut oil or butter
- 1/2 cup powdered erythritol (or sweetener of your choice)
- 1 large egg
- 1 teaspoon vanilla extract
- 1 1/4 cups almond flour
- 2 tablespoons coconut flour
- 1/2 teaspoon baking soda
- 1/4 teaspoon salt
- 1/2 cup sugar-free chocolate chips

Instructions:

1. **Preheat Oven**: Preheat your oven to 350°F (175°C). Line a baking sheet with parchment paper or a silicone baking mat.
2. **Prepare Zucchini**: Place the shredded zucchini in a clean kitchen towel or paper towel and squeeze out excess moisture. Set aside.
3. **Mix Wet Ingredients**: In a large bowl, whisk together melted coconut oil or butter, powdered erythritol, egg, and vanilla extract until well combined.
4. **Add Dry Ingredients**: Add almond flour, coconut flour, baking soda, and salt to the wet ingredients. Stir until a dough forms.
5. **Fold in Zucchini and Chocolate Chips**: Gently fold in the shredded zucchini and sugar-free chocolate chips until evenly distributed in the dough.
6. **Shape Cookies**: Using a spoon or cookie scoop, drop tablespoon-sized portions of dough onto the prepared baking sheet, spacing them about 2 inches apart. Flatten slightly with the back of a spoon or your fingers.
7. **Bake**: Bake in the preheated oven for 12-15 minutes, or until the edges are golden brown and the tops are set.
8. **Cool**: Allow the cookies to cool on the baking sheet for 5 minutes, then transfer them to a wire rack to cool completely.
9. **Serve**: Enjoy your soft and delicious Zucchini Chocolate Chip Cookies! Store leftovers in an airtight container at room temperature or in the refrigerator.

These cookies are a nutritious twist on traditional chocolate chip cookies, with added fiber from the zucchini and almond flour. They are low-carb and keto-friendly, making them a guilt-free treat for any occasion. Adjust the sweetness and chocolate chips to your liking for the perfect balance of flavors.

Creamy Sugar-Free Popsicles (Various Flavors)

Base Ingredients:

- 1 cup unsweetened almond milk (or any milk of your choice)
- 1 cup heavy cream (or coconut cream for dairy-free option)
- 1/4 cup powdered erythritol (adjust to taste)
- 1 teaspoon vanilla extract
- Pinch of salt

Flavor Options:

For Chocolate Popsicles:

- 2 tablespoons unsweetened cocoa powder

For Strawberry Popsicles:

- 1 cup fresh or frozen strawberries, pureed

For Matcha Green Tea Popsicles:

- 1 tablespoon matcha powder

For Coffee Popsicles:

- 1/2 cup brewed coffee, cooled

For Coconut Popsicles:

- 1/4 cup shredded coconut (optional)

Instructions:

1. **Prepare Base Mixture:**
   - In a blender, combine almond milk (or your choice of milk), heavy cream (or coconut cream), powdered erythritol, vanilla extract, and a pinch of salt. Blend until smooth.
2. **Customize Flavors:**
   - Depending on your chosen flavor:
     - **Chocolate Popsicles:** Add cocoa powder to the base mixture and blend until smooth.

- **Strawberry Popsicles:** Puree fresh or frozen strawberries separately, then mix into the base mixture.
- **Matcha Green Tea Popsicles:** Add matcha powder to the base mixture and blend until combined.
- **Coffee Popsicles:** Mix cooled brewed coffee into the base mixture.
- **Coconut Popsicles:** Add shredded coconut to the base mixture and blend until incorporated.

3. **Fill Popsicle Molds:**
   - Pour each flavored mixture into popsicle molds, dividing evenly. Leave a little space at the top for expansion.
4. **Insert Sticks and Freeze:**
   - Place popsicle sticks into each mold. Freeze for at least 4-6 hours, or until completely solid.
5. **Serve:**
   - To release the popsicles from the molds, run warm water over the outside of the molds for a few seconds. Gently pull out the popsicles and serve immediately.
6. **Enjoy:**
   - Enjoy your creamy sugar-free popsicles as a refreshing treat!

These creamy sugar-free popsicles are versatile and can be customized with endless flavor combinations. Adjust the sweetness to your taste by adding more or less powdered erythritol. They are perfect for satisfying cravings without the guilt of added sugars, making them suitable for those on a keto or low-carb diet. Experiment with different flavors and enjoy a cool and creamy dessert anytime!

Keto Chocolate Chip Cookie Dough Fat Bombs

Ingredients:

- 1/2 cup almond flour
- 1/4 cup powdered erythritol (or sweetener of your choice)
- 1/4 cup melted coconut oil
- 1/2 teaspoon vanilla extract
- Pinch of salt
- 1/4 cup sugar-free chocolate chips

Instructions:

1. **Mix Ingredients**: In a mixing bowl, combine almond flour, powdered erythritol, melted coconut oil, vanilla extract, and a pinch of salt. Stir until smooth and well combined.
2. **Add Chocolate Chips**: Fold in sugar-free chocolate chips until evenly distributed throughout the dough.
3. **Shape Dough**: Scoop out tablespoon-sized portions of the dough and roll them into balls between your palms. Place them on a parchment-lined baking sheet or plate.
4. **Chill**: Place the cookie dough balls in the refrigerator for about 30 minutes to firm up.
5. **Serve**: Enjoy your Keto Chocolate Chip Cookie Dough Fat Bombs as a satisfying snack or dessert.
6. **Store**: Store any leftovers in an airtight container in the refrigerator for up to one week, or freeze for longer storage.

These fat bombs are rich in healthy fats from almond flour and coconut oil, making them a great option for those following a ketogenic or low-carb diet. The addition of sugar-free chocolate chips adds a delightful chocolatey crunch without the extra carbs. Adjust the sweetness to your taste preference by adding more or less powdered erythritol. Enjoy these indulgent treats while staying on track with your low-carb goals!

Peanut Butter Chocolate Chip Mug Cake

Ingredients:

- 2 tablespoons almond flour
- 1 tablespoon powdered erythritol (or sweetener of your choice)
- 1 tablespoon cocoa powder
- 1/4 teaspoon baking powder
- Pinch of salt
- 1 tablespoon creamy peanut butter
- 1 tablespoon melted butter or coconut oil
- 1 tablespoon unsweetened almond milk (or any milk of your choice)
- 1/4 teaspoon vanilla extract
- 1 tablespoon sugar-free chocolate chips

Instructions:

1. **Prepare Mug**: Grease a microwave-safe mug with butter or cooking spray.
2. **Mix Dry Ingredients**: In the mug, whisk together almond flour, powdered erythritol, cocoa powder, baking powder, and a pinch of salt until well combined.
3. **Add Wet Ingredients**: Add creamy peanut butter, melted butter or coconut oil, unsweetened almond milk, and vanilla extract to the mug. Stir until smooth and no lumps remain.
4. **Add Chocolate Chips**: Gently fold in sugar-free chocolate chips into the batter.
5. **Microwave**: Microwave on high for 60-90 seconds, depending on your microwave's wattage. Check after 60 seconds; the cake should be firm to the touch and slightly risen.
6. **Serve**: Let the mug cake cool for a minute or two. Optionally, top with a dollop of whipped cream or a sprinkle of additional chocolate chips.
7. **Enjoy**: Grab a spoon and enjoy your warm and gooey Peanut Butter Chocolate Chip Mug Cake straight from the mug!

This mug cake is a perfect single-serving dessert or snack that's keto-friendly and low-carb. Adjust the sweetness to your taste preference by adding more or less powdered erythritol. It's quick to make and satisfies your chocolate and peanut butter cravings without derailing your diet goals.

Sugar-Free Coconut Cream Pie

Ingredients:

For the Crust:

- 1 1/2 cups almond flour
- 1/4 cup powdered erythritol (or sweetener of your choice)
- 1/4 cup melted coconut oil
- Pinch of salt

For the Coconut Cream Filling:

- 1 can (13.5 oz) full-fat coconut milk
- 1/2 cup unsweetened almond milk (or any milk of your choice)
- 1/3 cup powdered erythritol (adjust to taste)
- 1/4 cup coconut flour
- 3 large egg yolks
- 1 teaspoon vanilla extract
- 1 cup shredded unsweetened coconut flakes
- Pinch of salt

For the Whipped Cream Topping:

- 1 cup heavy cream (or coconut cream for dairy-free option)
- 1 tablespoon powdered erythritol (or sweetener of your choice)
- 1 teaspoon vanilla extract

Instructions:

For the Crust:

1. **Preheat Oven**: Preheat your oven to 350°F (175°C).
2. **Mix Crust Ingredients**: In a bowl, combine almond flour, powdered erythritol, melted coconut oil, and a pinch of salt. Mix until well combined and press into the bottom and up the sides of a 9-inch pie dish.
3. **Bake Crust**: Bake the crust in the preheated oven for 10-12 minutes, until golden brown. Remove from oven and let it cool completely.

For the Coconut Cream Filling:

1. **Prepare Coconut Milk**: In a saucepan, combine coconut milk and almond milk. Heat over medium heat until it starts to simmer.
2. **Mix Dry Ingredients**: In a separate bowl, whisk together powdered erythritol, coconut flour, and a pinch of salt.
3. **Temper Eggs**: In another bowl, whisk egg yolks. Gradually add a small amount of the heated coconut milk mixture to the egg yolks, whisking constantly, to temper the eggs.
4. **Combine and Cook**: Gradually whisk the tempered egg mixture back into the saucepan with the remaining coconut milk mixture. Cook over medium heat, stirring constantly, until the mixture thickens enough to coat the back of a spoon (about 5-7 minutes).
5. **Add Vanilla and Coconut**: Remove from heat and stir in vanilla extract and shredded coconut flakes.
6. **Cool and Fill**: Let the coconut cream filling cool slightly, then pour it into the cooled almond flour crust. Smooth the top with a spatula.
7. **Chill**: Refrigerate the pie for at least 4 hours, or until set and firm.

For the Whipped Cream Topping:

1. **Whip Cream**: In a mixing bowl, whip heavy cream (or coconut cream), powdered erythritol, and vanilla extract until stiff peaks form.
2. **Decorate**: Spread or pipe the whipped cream over the chilled pie.
3. **Serve**: Slice and serve your delicious Sugar-Free Coconut Cream Pie chilled.

This coconut cream pie is rich, creamy, and full of coconut flavor without any added sugars. It's a perfect dessert option for those following a keto or low-carb diet. Adjust the sweetness and coconut intensity to suit your taste preferences. Enjoy this guilt-free treat!

Lemon Coconut Energy Balls

Ingredients:

- 1 cup shredded coconut (unsweetened)
- Zest of 1 lemon
- Juice of 1 lemon
- 1 cup almond flour
- 1/4 cup powdered erythritol (or sweetener of your choice)
- 1/4 cup melted coconut oil
- 1 teaspoon vanilla extract
- Pinch of salt

Instructions:

1. **Prepare Ingredients**: In a food processor, combine shredded coconut and lemon zest. Pulse until the coconut is finely shredded and the zest is well incorporated.
2. **Add Remaining Ingredients**: Add almond flour, powdered erythritol, melted coconut oil, lemon juice, vanilla extract, and a pinch of salt to the food processor.
3. **Blend**: Pulse the mixture until it comes together into a sticky dough. You may need to scrape down the sides of the food processor bowl with a spatula and pulse again to ensure everything is well mixed.
4. **Form Balls**: Using your hands, scoop out tablespoon-sized portions of the mixture and roll them into balls between your palms. If the mixture is too sticky, wet your hands slightly with water before rolling.
5. **Chill**: Place the energy balls on a parchment-lined baking sheet or plate. Chill in the refrigerator for at least 30 minutes to firm up.
6. **Store**: Once chilled and firm, transfer the energy balls to an airtight container. Store in the refrigerator for up to 1 week, or freeze for longer storage.
7. **Serve**: Enjoy your Lemon Coconut Energy Balls as a quick and nutritious snack!

These energy balls are bursting with citrusy lemon flavor and the natural sweetness of coconut, making them a delightful treat. They are keto-friendly, gluten-free, and perfect for satisfying your sweet cravings while providing a boost of energy from healthy fats and protein. Adjust the sweetness to your taste by adding more or less powdered erythritol. Enjoy these delicious bites whenever you need a healthy pick-me-up!

Low-Carb Chocolate Avocado Truffles

Ingredients:

- 1 ripe avocado
- 1/4 cup cocoa powder (unsweetened)
- 2-3 tablespoons powdered erythritol (or sweetener of your choice), adjust to taste
- 1/2 teaspoon vanilla extract
- Pinch of salt
- 1/4 cup sugar-free dark chocolate chips or chopped sugar-free dark chocolate
- Unsweetened cocoa powder, shredded coconut, or chopped nuts for coating (optional)

Instructions:

1. **Prepare Avocado**: Cut the avocado in half, remove the pit, and scoop out the flesh into a bowl.
2. **Mash Avocado**: Use a fork to mash the avocado until smooth and creamy.
3. **Add Ingredients**: Add cocoa powder, powdered erythritol (start with 2 tablespoons and adjust sweetness to taste), vanilla extract, and a pinch of salt to the mashed avocado. Mix until well combined.
4. **Melt Chocolate**: In a microwave-safe bowl or over a double boiler, melt the sugar-free dark chocolate chips until smooth.
5. **Combine with Avocado Mixture**: Pour the melted chocolate into the avocado mixture. Stir until thoroughly combined and smooth.
6. **Chill**: Place the mixture in the refrigerator for about 30 minutes to firm up slightly.
7. **Shape Truffles**: Once chilled, scoop out tablespoon-sized portions of the mixture and roll them into balls between your palms. If the mixture is too sticky, dust your hands with cocoa powder or chill the mixture longer.
8. **Coat Truffles (Optional)**: Roll the truffles in unsweetened cocoa powder, shredded coconut, or chopped nuts for coating, if desired.
9. **Chill Again**: Place the coated truffles on a plate or baking sheet lined with parchment paper. Chill in the refrigerator for at least 1 hour to firm up.
10. **Serve**: Enjoy your Low-Carb Chocolate Avocado Truffles chilled as a delicious and healthy dessert or snack!

These truffles are rich in flavor and healthy fats from avocado, making them a satisfying treat for those on a low-carb or keto diet. They are also packed with antioxidants from cocoa powder and are naturally sweetened with erythritol. Customize the recipe by adjusting the sweetness level or experimenting with different coatings for variety.

Almond Flour Shortbread Cookies

Ingredients:

- 1 1/2 cups almond flour
- 1/4 cup powdered erythritol (or sweetener of your choice)
- 1/4 teaspoon salt
- 1/2 cup unsalted butter, softened (or coconut oil for dairy-free option)
- 1 teaspoon vanilla extract

Instructions:

1. **Preheat Oven**: Preheat your oven to 350°F (175°C). Line a baking sheet with parchment paper.
2. **Mix Dry Ingredients**: In a mixing bowl, combine almond flour, powdered erythritol, and salt.
3. **Add Butter and Vanilla**: Add softened butter (or coconut oil) and vanilla extract to the dry ingredients.
4. **Mix Until Dough Forms**: Use a fork or your hands to mix everything together until a dough forms. It should be crumbly but hold together when pressed.
5. **Shape Cookies**: Take tablespoon-sized portions of dough and roll them into balls. Place them on the prepared baking sheet. Use a fork to gently flatten each ball into a cookie shape, creating a crosshatch pattern if desired.
6. **Bake**: Bake in the preheated oven for 10-12 minutes, or until the edges are golden brown.
7. **Cool**: Allow the cookies to cool on the baking sheet for 5 minutes, then transfer them to a wire rack to cool completely.
8. **Serve**: Enjoy your almond flour shortbread cookies with a cup of tea or coffee!

These cookies are buttery, crumbly, and perfectly sweetened with erythritol. They are a wonderful treat for those following a low-carb or keto diet, and they can be easily customized with additions like lemon zest, cinnamon, or chopped nuts. Store any leftovers in an airtight container at room temperature for up to a week, or freeze for longer storage.

Sugar-Free Raspberry Coconut Squares

Ingredients:

For the Base:

- 1 cup almond flour
- 1/4 cup powdered erythritol (or sweetener of your choice)
- 1/4 cup melted butter
- 1/2 teaspoon vanilla extract
- Pinch of salt

For the Raspberry Layer:

- 1 1/2 cups fresh or frozen raspberries
- 2 tablespoons water
- 2 tablespoons powdered erythritol (adjust to taste)
- 1 tablespoon chia seeds

For the Coconut Topping:

- 1 cup shredded unsweetened coconut
- 1/4 cup melted coconut oil
- 2 tablespoons powdered erythritol (or sweetener of your choice)
- 1/2 teaspoon vanilla extract

Instructions:

1. Prepare the Base:

- Preheat your oven to 350°F (175°C). Line an 8x8 inch baking dish with parchment paper.
- In a bowl, mix together almond flour, powdered erythritol, melted butter, vanilla extract, and a pinch of salt until well combined.
- Press the mixture evenly into the bottom of the lined baking dish.
- Bake for 10-12 minutes, or until the edges are lightly golden. Remove from the oven and let it cool slightly.

2. Make the Raspberry Layer:

- In a small saucepan, combine raspberries, water, and powdered erythritol over medium heat.

- Cook, stirring occasionally, until raspberries break down and become saucy (about 5-7 minutes).
- Remove from heat and stir in chia seeds. Let it sit for 5-10 minutes to thicken.
- Spread the raspberry mixture evenly over the cooled almond flour base.

3. Prepare the Coconut Topping:

- In a bowl, combine shredded coconut, melted coconut oil, powdered erythritol, and vanilla extract. Mix until well combined.
- Spread the coconut topping evenly over the raspberry layer.

4. Chill and Serve:

- Refrigerate the assembled squares for at least 2 hours, or until firm.
- Once chilled, lift the parchment paper to remove the squares from the baking dish. Cut into squares and serve.

These Sugar-Free Raspberry Coconut Squares are a delightful combination of tangy raspberries and sweet coconut, perfect for a keto-friendly dessert or snack. They can be stored in an airtight container in the refrigerator for up to a week. Enjoy these guilt-free treats whenever you crave a delicious and satisfying snack!

Pumpkin Spice Energy Bites

Ingredients:

- 1 cup almond flour
- 1/2 cup canned pumpkin puree
- 1/4 cup powdered erythritol (or sweetener of your choice)
- 1/4 cup almond butter (or any nut butter of your choice)
- 1 teaspoon pumpkin pie spice
- 1/2 teaspoon vanilla extract
- Pinch of salt
- Optional: 1/4 cup sugar-free chocolate chips or chopped nuts for added texture

Instructions:

1. **Mix Ingredients**: In a mixing bowl, combine almond flour, canned pumpkin puree, powdered erythritol, almond butter, pumpkin pie spice, vanilla extract, and a pinch of salt. Mix until well combined and smooth.
2. **Add Optional Ingredients**: If desired, fold in sugar-free chocolate chips or chopped nuts for added texture and flavor.
3. **Shape into Bites**: Scoop out tablespoon-sized portions of the mixture and roll them into balls between your palms. If the mixture is too sticky, wet your hands slightly with water before rolling.
4. **Chill**: Place the energy bites on a parchment-lined baking sheet or plate. Chill in the refrigerator for at least 30 minutes to firm up.
5. **Serve**: Enjoy your Pumpkin Spice Energy Bites chilled as a nutritious snack or dessert!

These energy bites are packed with pumpkin flavor and warm spices, making them perfect for the fall season or any time you crave a healthy treat. They are low-carb, keto-friendly, and rich in healthy fats and fiber from almond flour and nut butter. Store any leftovers in an airtight container in the refrigerator for up to one week, or freeze for longer storage. Enjoy these tasty bites whenever you need a quick burst of energy!

Keto Chocolate Peanut Butter Cups

Ingredients:

For the Chocolate Shell:

- 6 oz sugar-free dark chocolate or sugar-free chocolate chips
- 1 tablespoon coconut oil

For the Peanut Butter Filling:

- 1/2 cup creamy peanut butter (or almond butter for variation)
- 2 tablespoons powdered erythritol (or sweetener of your choice)
- 2 tablespoons coconut flour
- 1/2 teaspoon vanilla extract
- Pinch of salt

Instructions:

1. **Prepare Muffin Tin:**
   - Line a muffin tin with 12 paper or silicone muffin liners.
2. **Melt Chocolate:**
   - In a microwave-safe bowl or over a double boiler, melt the sugar-free dark chocolate (or chocolate chips) and coconut oil together until smooth. Stir until well combined.
3. **Coat Muffin Liners:**
   - Spoon a small amount of melted chocolate into each muffin liner, just enough to cover the bottom. Use the back of a spoon or a small brush to spread the chocolate up the sides of the liners to create a shell. Place the muffin tin in the freezer for 10-15 minutes to set.
4. **Prepare Peanut Butter Filling:**
   - In a separate bowl, mix together creamy peanut butter (or almond butter), powdered erythritol, coconut flour, vanilla extract, and a pinch of salt until smooth and well combined.
5. **Fill Chocolate Cups:**
   - Remove the muffin tin from the freezer. Spoon a small amount of the peanut butter filling into each chocolate cup, spreading it out evenly.
6. **Top with Chocolate:**
   - Pour the remaining melted chocolate over the peanut butter filling in each cup, covering it completely and smoothing the tops with a spoon.

7. **Chill:**
   - Return the muffin tin to the freezer for another 15-20 minutes, or until the chocolate is set.
8. **Serve:**
   - Once set, remove the Keto Chocolate Peanut Butter Cups from the muffin tin and enjoy! Store any leftovers in an airtight container in the refrigerator.

These Keto Chocolate Peanut Butter Cups are rich, creamy, and perfectly sweetened without any added sugars. They make a fantastic treat for those following a low-carb or ketogenic diet, and they're sure to satisfy your chocolate cravings. Customize them by using different nut butters or adding chopped nuts for extra crunch. Enjoy these delicious cups guilt-free!

No-Bake Sugar-Free Key Lime Pie

Ingredients:

For the Crust:

- 1 1/2 cups almond flour
- 1/4 cup powdered erythritol (or sweetener of your choice)
- 1/4 cup melted coconut oil
- Pinch of salt

For the Filling:

- 1 can (14 oz) coconut cream or full-fat coconut milk, chilled
- 1/2 cup fresh lime juice (about 4-5 limes)
- Zest of 2 limes
- 1/4 cup powdered erythritol (adjust to taste)
- 1 teaspoon vanilla extract
- Green food coloring (optional, for color)

For Garnish (optional):

- Whipped cream (using heavy cream and powdered erythritol)
- Lime slices or zest

Instructions:

1. Prepare the Crust:

- In a mixing bowl, combine almond flour, powdered erythritol, melted coconut oil, and a pinch of salt. Mix until well combined and the mixture resembles coarse crumbs.
- Press the crust mixture evenly into the bottom and up the sides of a 9-inch pie dish. Use the back of a spoon or your hands to compact it firmly. Place the crust in the refrigerator while you prepare the filling.

2. Make the Filling:

- In a large bowl, scoop out the chilled coconut cream or the solid part of chilled coconut milk (discard the liquid or save for another use). Beat the coconut cream with a hand mixer or stand mixer until fluffy.

- Add fresh lime juice, lime zest, powdered erythritol, vanilla extract, and green food coloring (if using) to the whipped coconut cream. Mix until smooth and well combined. Adjust sweetness to taste by adding more powdered erythritol if needed.

3. Assemble the Pie:

- Pour the lime filling into the prepared crust, spreading it out evenly with a spatula.
- Smooth the top with the back of a spoon or an offset spatula.

4. Chill:

- Refrigerate the Key Lime Pie for at least 4 hours, or until set and firm.

5. Garnish and Serve:

- Before serving, optionally garnish with whipped cream, lime slices, or additional lime zest.

6. Enjoy:

- Slice and serve your delicious No-Bake Sugar-Free Key Lime Pie chilled.

This pie is creamy, tangy, and bursting with citrus flavor, making it a perfect dessert for any occasion. It's keto-friendly, gluten-free, and low in carbs, making it suitable for those following a low-carb or ketogenic diet. Store any leftovers in the refrigerator for up to 3-4 days. Enjoy this refreshing and guilt-free dessert!

Blueberry Almond Scones

Ingredients:

- 2 cups almond flour
- 1/4 cup powdered erythritol (or sweetener of your choice)
- 1 teaspoon baking powder
- 1/4 teaspoon salt
- 1/4 cup cold unsalted butter, cut into small pieces
- 1/4 cup unsweetened almond milk (or any milk of your choice)
- 1 large egg
- 1 teaspoon vanilla extract
- 1/2 cup fresh or frozen blueberries
- Zest of 1 lemon (optional, for extra flavor)

Instructions:

1. **Preheat Oven**: Preheat your oven to 350°F (175°C). Line a baking sheet with parchment paper.
2. **Mix Dry Ingredients**: In a large mixing bowl, whisk together almond flour, powdered erythritol, baking powder, and salt.
3. **Cut in Butter**: Using a pastry cutter or fork, cut the cold butter pieces into the almond flour mixture until it resembles coarse crumbs.
4. **Add Wet Ingredients**: In a separate bowl, whisk together almond milk, egg, and vanilla extract.
5. **Combine and Form Dough**: Pour the wet ingredients into the almond flour mixture. Stir until just combined. Gently fold in the blueberries and lemon zest, being careful not to crush the berries.
6. **Shape Scones**: Transfer the dough onto the prepared baking sheet. Pat the dough into a circle about 1 inch thick.
7. **Cut into Triangles**: Use a sharp knife to cut the dough into 8 equal triangles, like pizza slices.
8. **Bake**: Bake in the preheated oven for 18-20 minutes, or until the scones are golden brown and cooked through.
9. **Cool**: Allow the scones to cool on the baking sheet for a few minutes, then transfer them to a wire rack to cool completely.
10. **Serve**: Enjoy your Blueberry Almond Scones warm or at room temperature.

These scones are tender, flavorful, and packed with juicy blueberries. They are low-carb and suitable for those following a keto or gluten-free diet. Store any leftovers in an airtight container at room temperature for up to 3 days, or freeze for longer storage. Enjoy these delicious scones for breakfast, brunch, or as a delightful snack with your favorite beverage!

Sugar-Free Greek Yogurt Parfait

Ingredients:

- 2 cups plain Greek yogurt (full-fat or low-fat)
- 1/4 cup powdered erythritol (or sweetener of your choice, adjust to taste)
- 1 teaspoon vanilla extract
- 1 cup fresh berries (such as strawberries, blueberries, raspberries, or blackberries)
- 1/2 cup granola (sugar-free or low-carb if desired)
- 1/4 cup chopped nuts (such as almonds, walnuts, or pecans)
- Optional: 1 tablespoon chia seeds or flaxseeds

Instructions:

1. **Prepare Yogurt**: In a mixing bowl, combine the plain Greek yogurt, powdered erythritol, and vanilla extract. Mix well until the sweetener is fully incorporated and the yogurt is smooth.
2. **Layer the Parfait**:
    - **First Layer**: Spoon a generous amount of the sweetened Greek yogurt into the bottom of each serving glass or bowl.
    - **Second Layer**: Add a layer of fresh berries on top of the yogurt.
    - **Third Layer**: Sprinkle a layer of granola over the berries.
    - **Fourth Layer**: Add a layer of chopped nuts.
3. **Repeat Layers**: Repeat the layers, starting with the yogurt, until you reach the top of your serving glass or bowl. Finish with a topping of fresh berries, granola, and chopped nuts.
4. **Optional Toppings**: Sprinkle chia seeds or flaxseeds on top for added nutrition and texture.
5. **Serve**: Serve immediately or refrigerate until ready to enjoy. The parfait can be stored in the refrigerator for up to 2 days.

Tips:

- **Customize It**: Feel free to customize your parfait with your favorite fruits, nuts, or seeds. You can also add a drizzle of sugar-free syrup or a dollop of sugar-free fruit preserves for extra flavor.
- **Layering**: For a more visual appeal, use clear glasses or mason jars to show off the beautiful layers.

This Sugar-Free Greek Yogurt Parfait is a refreshing and healthy option that provides protein, healthy fats, and fiber. It's perfect for a quick breakfast, snack, or even a light dessert. Enjoy!

Chocolate Hazelnut Fat Bombs

Ingredients:

- 1/2 cup hazelnut butter (or any nut butter of your choice)
- 1/4 cup coconut oil
- 1/4 cup unsweetened cocoa powder
- 2 tablespoons powdered erythritol (or sweetener of your choice, adjust to taste)
- 1/2 teaspoon vanilla extract
- Pinch of salt
- Optional: 1/4 cup chopped hazelnuts for added texture

Instructions:

1. **Melt Ingredients**: In a microwave-safe bowl or over a double boiler, combine hazelnut butter and coconut oil. Heat until melted and smooth, stirring occasionally.
2. **Mix In Cocoa**: Add unsweetened cocoa powder, powdered erythritol, vanilla extract, and a pinch of salt to the melted mixture. Stir until well combined and smooth.
3. **Add Optional Nuts**: If using, fold in the chopped hazelnuts for added texture.
4. **Fill Molds**: Pour the mixture into silicone molds or ice cube trays, filling each cavity about 3/4 full. You can also use mini muffin liners if you don't have silicone molds.
5. **Chill**: Place the molds in the refrigerator or freezer for at least 1 hour, or until the fat bombs are firm.
6. **Remove from Molds**: Once firm, pop the fat bombs out of the molds.
7. **Store**: Store the fat bombs in an airtight container in the refrigerator or freezer. They will keep for up to 2 weeks in the fridge and longer in the freezer.
8. **Serve**: Enjoy your Chocolate Hazelnut Fat Bombs straight from the fridge or freezer for a quick and satisfying keto treat!

These fat bombs are rich, chocolaty, and have a wonderful nutty flavor from the hazelnut butter. They are perfect for a quick energy boost, a snack, or a dessert that fits into your low-carb or ketogenic diet. Adjust the sweetness to your liking, and feel free to experiment with different nut butters and add-ins for variety. Enjoy!

Vanilla Almond Flour Cake

Ingredients:

For the Cake:

- 2 1/2 cups almond flour
- 1/4 cup coconut flour
- 1 cup powdered erythritol (or sweetener of your choice)
- 1 teaspoon baking powder
- 1/2 teaspoon baking soda
- 1/4 teaspoon salt
- 4 large eggs
- 1/2 cup unsalted butter, melted (or coconut oil for dairy-free option)
- 1/2 cup unsweetened almond milk (or any milk of your choice)
- 1 tablespoon vanilla extract
- 1 teaspoon apple cider vinegar

For the Frosting (optional):

- 1/2 cup unsalted butter, softened (or coconut cream for dairy-free option)
- 1 cup powdered erythritol (or sweetener of your choice)
- 2 teaspoons vanilla extract
- 2-3 tablespoons heavy cream (or coconut milk for dairy-free option)

Instructions:

1. Preheat Oven and Prepare Pan:

- Preheat your oven to 350°F (175°C). Grease an 8-inch round cake pan and line the bottom with parchment paper.

2. Mix Dry Ingredients:

- In a large mixing bowl, combine almond flour, coconut flour, powdered erythritol, baking powder, baking soda, and salt. Mix well.

3. Mix Wet Ingredients:

- In another bowl, whisk together the eggs, melted butter, almond milk, vanilla extract, and apple cider vinegar until well combined.

4. Combine Wet and Dry Ingredients:

- Pour the wet ingredients into the dry ingredients. Stir until just combined and smooth. Do not overmix.

5. Bake the Cake:

- Pour the batter into the prepared cake pan and spread it evenly.
- Bake in the preheated oven for 30-35 minutes, or until a toothpick inserted into the center of the cake comes out clean.
- Let the cake cool in the pan for 10 minutes, then transfer it to a wire rack to cool completely.

6. Prepare the Frosting (if using):

- In a mixing bowl, beat the softened butter until creamy.
- Gradually add the powdered erythritol and continue to beat until smooth and fluffy.
- Add the vanilla extract and heavy cream, and beat until the frosting reaches a spreadable consistency.

7. Frost the Cake:

- Once the cake is completely cool, spread the frosting evenly over the top and sides of the cake.

8. Serve:

- Slice and serve your Vanilla Almond Flour Cake. Enjoy!

Tips:

- **Storage**: Store any leftover cake in an airtight container in the refrigerator for up to 5 days. Bring to room temperature before serving for the best texture.
- **Add-ins**: For variety, you can add sugar-free chocolate chips, berries, or chopped nuts to the batter before baking.
- **Layer Cake**: If you'd like to make a layer cake, double the recipe and divide the batter between two 8-inch cake pans. Frost between the layers and on top.

This Vanilla Almond Flour Cake is moist, flavorful, and perfect for those following a low-carb or gluten-free diet. Enjoy it plain or with the optional frosting for a special treat!

Keto Pecan Pie Bars

Ingredients:

For the Crust:

- 2 cups almond flour
- 1/4 cup powdered erythritol (or sweetener of your choice)
- 1/4 cup unsalted butter, melted
- 1 teaspoon vanilla extract
- Pinch of salt

For the Pecan Filling:

- 3 large eggs
- 1 cup powdered erythritol (or sweetener of your choice)
- 1/2 cup unsalted butter, melted
- 1 tablespoon vanilla extract
- 1 1/2 cups pecans, roughly chopped
- 1/2 teaspoon salt

Instructions:

1. Preheat Oven and Prepare Pan:

- Preheat your oven to 350°F (175°C). Line an 8x8 inch baking pan with parchment paper, leaving some overhang for easy removal.

2. Make the Crust:

- In a mixing bowl, combine almond flour, powdered erythritol, melted butter, vanilla extract, and a pinch of salt. Mix until well combined.
- Press the mixture evenly into the bottom of the prepared baking pan.
- Bake in the preheated oven for 10-12 minutes, or until the edges are lightly golden. Remove from the oven and let it cool slightly.

3. Prepare the Pecan Filling:

- In a large mixing bowl, whisk together the eggs, powdered erythritol, melted butter, vanilla extract, and salt until smooth.
- Stir in the chopped pecans until well coated.

4. Assemble and Bake:

- Pour the pecan filling over the pre-baked crust, spreading it out evenly.
- Bake in the oven for 25-30 minutes, or until the filling is set and the top is golden brown.

5. Cool and Serve:

- Allow the bars to cool completely in the pan on a wire rack. Once cool, use the parchment paper overhang to lift the bars out of the pan.
- Cut into squares or bars and serve.

Tips:

- **Storage**: Store the bars in an airtight container in the refrigerator for up to one week. They can also be frozen for longer storage.
- **Serving**: These bars are delicious served chilled or at room temperature. For an extra treat, top with a dollop of sugar-free whipped cream.
- **Variations**: You can add a pinch of cinnamon or a splash of bourbon to the filling for a flavor twist.

Enjoy your Keto Pecan Pie Bars as a tasty low-carb dessert or snack!

Sugar-Free Apple Cinnamon Muffins

Ingredients:

- 2 cups almond flour
- 1/4 cup coconut flour
- 1/2 cup powdered erythritol (or sweetener of your choice)
- 1 tablespoon cinnamon
- 1 teaspoon baking powder
- 1/2 teaspoon baking soda
- 1/4 teaspoon salt
- 3 large eggs
- 1/2 cup unsweetened applesauce
- 1/4 cup unsweetened almond milk (or any milk of your choice)
- 1/4 cup melted coconut oil (or unsalted butter, melted)
- 1 teaspoon vanilla extract
- 1 medium apple, peeled, cored, and finely chopped

Instructions:

1. Preheat Oven and Prepare Pan:

- Preheat your oven to 350°F (175°C). Line a 12-cup muffin tin with paper liners or grease the tin well.

2. Mix Dry Ingredients:

- In a large mixing bowl, whisk together almond flour, coconut flour, powdered erythritol, cinnamon, baking powder, baking soda, and salt.

3. Mix Wet Ingredients:

- In another bowl, whisk together the eggs, unsweetened applesauce, almond milk, melted coconut oil, and vanilla extract until well combined.

4. Combine Wet and Dry Ingredients:

- Pour the wet ingredients into the dry ingredients and stir until just combined. Do not overmix.
- Gently fold in the chopped apple pieces.

5. Fill Muffin Tin:

- Divide the batter evenly among the 12 muffin cups, filling each about 3/4 full.

6. Bake:

- Bake in the preheated oven for 20-25 minutes, or until a toothpick inserted into the center of a muffin comes out clean.
- Let the muffins cool in the tin for about 10 minutes, then transfer them to a wire rack to cool completely.

7. Serve:

- Enjoy your Sugar-Free Apple Cinnamon Muffins warm or at room temperature. They are perfect for breakfast, snacks, or dessert.

Tips:

- **Storage**: Store any leftover muffins in an airtight container at room temperature for up to 2 days, or refrigerate for up to a week. They can also be frozen for longer storage.
- **Add-Ins**: For added texture and flavor, consider adding 1/4 cup of chopped nuts (such as walnuts or pecans) or a handful of sugar-free chocolate chips to the batter.
- **Spices**: If you like, add a pinch of nutmeg or allspice to the dry ingredients for an extra flavor boost.

These Sugar-Free Apple Cinnamon Muffins are moist, flavorful, and perfect for anyone looking for a healthier, low-carb muffin option. Enjoy!

Avocado Lime Cheesecake Bites

Ingredients:

For the Crust:

- 1 cup almond flour
- 2 tablespoons powdered erythritol (or sweetener of your choice)
- 1/4 cup melted coconut oil
- Pinch of salt

For the Filling:

- 2 ripe avocados, peeled and pitted
- 8 oz cream cheese, softened
- 1/2 cup powdered erythritol (or sweetener of your choice)
- 1/4 cup fresh lime juice (about 2-3 limes)
- Zest of 2 limes
- 1 teaspoon vanilla extract

Instructions:

1. Prepare the Crust:

- In a mixing bowl, combine almond flour, powdered erythritol, melted coconut oil, and a pinch of salt. Mix until well combined.
- Press the mixture evenly into the bottom of a lined mini muffin tin or silicone mold. Use the back of a spoon or your fingers to compact it firmly.
- Place the crusts in the refrigerator to set while you prepare the filling.

2. Prepare the Filling:

- In a food processor or blender, combine the avocados, softened cream cheese, powdered erythritol, fresh lime juice, lime zest, and vanilla extract. Blend until smooth and creamy.

3. Assemble the Cheesecake Bites:

- Spoon the avocado lime filling over the chilled crusts, filling each cavity to the top.
- Smooth the tops with a spatula or the back of a spoon.

4. Chill:

- Place the cheesecake bites in the refrigerator for at least 4 hours, or until set and firm. For quicker setting, you can place them in the freezer for about 1-2 hours.

5. Serve:

- Once set, remove the cheesecake bites from the molds. If using a silicone mold, gently push from the bottom to pop them out.
- Garnish with additional lime zest or a small lime slice if desired.

Tips:

- **Storage**: Store any leftover cheesecake bites in an airtight container in the refrigerator for up to 5 days, or freeze for longer storage.
- **Serving**: These bites are best served chilled for a refreshing and creamy treat.
- **Adjust Sweetness**: Taste the filling before assembling and adjust the sweetness according to your preference by adding more powdered erythritol if needed.

These Avocado Lime Cheesecake Bites are creamy, tangy, and packed with healthy fats, making them a perfect low-carb, keto-friendly dessert. Enjoy!

Almond Butter Chocolate Fudge

Ingredients:

- 1 cup almond butter (smooth or chunky)
- 1/2 cup coconut oil
- 1/2 cup unsweetened cocoa powder
- 1/4 cup powdered erythritol (or sweetener of your choice)
- 1 teaspoon vanilla extract
- Pinch of salt
- Optional: 1/4 cup chopped almonds or other nuts for added texture

Instructions:

1. Prepare the Pan:

- Line a small baking dish (8x8 inches works well) with parchment paper, leaving some overhang for easy removal.

2. Melt Ingredients:

- In a medium saucepan over low heat, combine the almond butter and coconut oil. Stir until melted and smooth.

3. Mix in Cocoa and Sweetener:

- Remove the saucepan from heat. Add the unsweetened cocoa powder, powdered erythritol, vanilla extract, and a pinch of salt. Stir until well combined and smooth.

4. Add Optional Nuts:

- If using, fold in the chopped almonds or other nuts for added texture.

5. Pour into Pan:

- Pour the mixture into the prepared baking dish, spreading it out evenly with a spatula.

6. Chill:

- Place the baking dish in the refrigerator for at least 2 hours, or until the fudge is set and firm.

7. Cut into Squares:

- Once set, use the parchment paper overhang to lift the fudge out of the pan. Cut into small squares or rectangles.

8. Serve:

- Enjoy your Almond Butter Chocolate Fudge chilled.

Tips:

- **Storage**: Store the fudge in an airtight container in the refrigerator for up to 2 weeks, or freeze for longer storage.
- **Serving**: This fudge is best served straight from the refrigerator, as it can soften at room temperature.
- **Variations**: Feel free to experiment with different nut butters (such as peanut butter or cashew butter) and add-ins (like sugar-free chocolate chips, shredded coconut, or seeds).

This Almond Butter Chocolate Fudge is rich, creamy, and perfectly sweetened without any added sugars. It's a great low-carb, keto-friendly treat that you can enjoy anytime. Enjoy!

Raspberry Almond Flour Blondies

Ingredients:

- 2 cups almond flour
- 1/2 cup powdered erythritol (or sweetener of your choice)
- 1/2 teaspoon baking soda
- 1/4 teaspoon salt
- 1/2 cup unsalted butter, melted (or coconut oil for dairy-free option)
- 2 large eggs
- 1 teaspoon vanilla extract
- 1/2 cup fresh or frozen raspberries
- 1/4 cup sliced almonds (optional, for topping)

Instructions:

1. Preheat Oven and Prepare Pan:

- Preheat your oven to 350°F (175°C). Line an 8x8 inch baking pan with parchment paper, leaving some overhang for easy removal.

2. Mix Dry Ingredients:

- In a large mixing bowl, whisk together the almond flour, powdered erythritol, baking soda, and salt until well combined.

3. Mix Wet Ingredients:

- In another bowl, whisk together the melted butter, eggs, and vanilla extract until smooth and well combined.

4. Combine Wet and Dry Ingredients:

- Pour the wet ingredients into the dry ingredients. Stir until just combined. Be careful not to overmix.

5. Add Raspberries:

- Gently fold in the raspberries, being careful not to crush them too much.

6. Pour Batter into Pan:

- Pour the batter into the prepared baking pan and spread it out evenly with a spatula.
- If using, sprinkle the sliced almonds on top of the batter.

7. Bake:

- Bake in the preheated oven for 25-30 minutes, or until the blondies are set and a toothpick inserted into the center comes out clean.

8. Cool and Cut:

- Allow the blondies to cool completely in the pan on a wire rack. Once cool, use the parchment paper overhang to lift them out of the pan.
- Cut into squares or rectangles.

9. Serve:

- Enjoy your Raspberry Almond Flour Blondies at room temperature or slightly chilled.

Tips:

- **Storage**: Store any leftover blondies in an airtight container in the refrigerator for up to a week. They can also be frozen for longer storage.
- **Variations**: You can substitute the raspberries with other berries, such as blueberries or blackberries. You can also add sugar-free chocolate chips or chopped nuts for extra texture and flavor.
- **Sweetness**: Adjust the sweetness to your taste by adding more or less powdered erythritol.

These Raspberry Almond Flour Blondies are moist, flavorful, and perfect for a healthy, low-carb dessert. Enjoy!

Sugar-Free Matcha Chia Pudding

Ingredients:

- 2 cups unsweetened almond milk (or any milk of your choice)
- 1/4 cup chia seeds
- 1-2 teaspoons matcha green tea powder (adjust to taste)
- 2-3 tablespoons powdered erythritol (or sweetener of your choice, adjust to taste)
- 1 teaspoon vanilla extract

Instructions:

1. Combine Ingredients:

- In a medium mixing bowl, whisk together the almond milk, matcha green tea powder, powdered erythritol, and vanilla extract until the matcha is fully dissolved and the mixture is smooth.

2. Add Chia Seeds:

- Add the chia seeds to the bowl and stir well to combine. Make sure the chia seeds are evenly distributed in the liquid.

3. Rest and Stir:

- Let the mixture sit for about 10-15 minutes, then stir again to break up any clumps of chia seeds that may have formed.

4. Refrigerate:

- Cover the bowl and refrigerate for at least 2 hours, or overnight, until the chia seeds have absorbed the liquid and the pudding has thickened.

5. Serve:

- Once the pudding has set, give it a good stir. Divide the pudding into individual serving bowls or jars.

6. Optional Toppings:

- Top with your favorite sugar-free toppings such as fresh berries, coconut flakes, or a drizzle of sugar-free syrup.

Tips:

- **Adjust Sweetness**: Taste the mixture before refrigerating and adjust the sweetness to your preference by adding more powdered erythritol if needed.
- **Consistency**: If the pudding is too thick after setting, you can stir in a little more almond milk to reach your desired consistency.
- **Matcha Quality**: Use a high-quality matcha powder for the best flavor and vibrant green color.
- **Storage**: Store any leftover pudding in an airtight container in the refrigerator for up to 5 days.

Enjoy this Sugar-Free Matcha Chia Pudding as a nutritious and energizing start to your day or a satisfying snack!

No-Bake Coconut Lime Energy Bites

Ingredients:

- 1 cup unsweetened shredded coconut
- 1/2 cup almond flour
- 1/4 cup powdered erythritol (or sweetener of your choice)
- Zest of 2 limes
- Juice of 1 lime
- 2 tablespoons coconut oil, melted
- 1 teaspoon vanilla extract
- Pinch of salt

Instructions:

1. Combine Dry Ingredients:

- In a medium mixing bowl, combine the unsweetened shredded coconut, almond flour, powdered erythritol, lime zest, and a pinch of salt. Mix well.

2. Add Wet Ingredients:

- Add the lime juice, melted coconut oil, and vanilla extract to the dry ingredients. Stir until everything is well combined and forms a sticky dough.

3. Form Energy Bites:

- Using your hands or a small cookie scoop, form the mixture into small balls (about 1 inch in diameter). Press firmly so they hold together.

4. Chill:

- Place the energy bites on a plate or a baking sheet lined with parchment paper. Refrigerate for at least 1 hour to firm up.

5. Serve:

- Enjoy your No-Bake Coconut Lime Energy Bites chilled. They are perfect for a quick snack or a burst of energy on the go.

Tips:

- **Storage**: Store any leftover energy bites in an airtight container in the refrigerator for up to a week. They can also be frozen for longer storage.
- **Variations**: You can add a tablespoon of chia seeds or flaxseeds for added nutrition and texture. For a more indulgent treat, you can dip the energy bites in melted sugar-free chocolate and let them set.
- **Sweetness**: Adjust the sweetness to your taste by adding more or less powdered erythritol.

These No-Bake Coconut Lime Energy Bites are refreshing, tangy, and packed with healthy fats and fiber, making them a perfect snack to keep you energized throughout the day. Enjoy!

Keto Chocolate Mint Cookies

Ingredients:

- 1 cup almond flour
- 1/4 cup cocoa powder (unsweetened)
- 1/2 cup powdered erythritol (or sweetener of your choice)
- 1/4 teaspoon salt
- 1/4 teaspoon baking soda
- 1/4 cup unsalted butter, softened
- 1 large egg
- 1/2 teaspoon peppermint extract
- 1/2 cup sugar-free chocolate chips or chopped dark chocolate

Instructions:

1. Preheat Oven:

- Preheat your oven to 350°F (175°C). Line a baking sheet with parchment paper or a silicone baking mat.

2. Mix Dry Ingredients:

- In a medium bowl, whisk together almond flour, cocoa powder, powdered erythritol, salt, and baking soda until well combined.

3. Cream Butter and Sweetener:

- In a separate bowl, cream together the softened butter and powdered erythritol until light and fluffy.

4. Add Wet Ingredients:

- Beat in the egg and peppermint extract until well combined.

5. Combine Wet and Dry Ingredients:

- Gradually add the dry ingredients to the wet ingredients, mixing until a dough forms. Fold in the sugar-free chocolate chips or chopped chocolate.

6. Form Cookies:

- Scoop tablespoon-sized portions of dough and roll them into balls. Place them on the prepared baking sheet, spacing them about 2 inches apart.

7. Flatten Cookies (Optional):

- Flatten each cookie slightly with the palm of your hand or the back of a spoon.

8. Bake:

- Bake in the preheated oven for 10-12 minutes, or until the edges are set. The cookies will still be soft in the center but will firm up as they cool.

9. Cool and Serve:

- Allow the cookies to cool on the baking sheet for 5 minutes, then transfer them to a wire rack to cool completely.

10. Enjoy:

- Once cooled, enjoy your Keto Chocolate Mint Cookies! Store any leftovers in an airtight container at room temperature for up to 5 days.

Tips:

- **Peppermint Extract**: Adjust the amount of peppermint extract to your preference. Start with 1/2 teaspoon and add more if you prefer a stronger mint flavor.
- **Chocolate Chips**: Ensure your chocolate chips or chopped chocolate are sugar-free to keep the cookies keto-friendly.
- **Variations**: For extra indulgence, drizzle melted sugar-free chocolate over the cooled cookies or sandwich them with a sugar-free mint filling.

These Keto Chocolate Mint Cookies are rich, chocolatey, and minty—a perfect combination for a low-carb treat! Enjoy them with a cup of coffee or as an after-dinner dessert.

Peanut Butter Banana Smoothie (Sweetened with Stevia)

Ingredients:

- 1 ripe banana, peeled and sliced
- 1 tablespoon natural peanut butter (unsweetened)
- 1 cup unsweetened almond milk (or any milk of your choice)
- 1/2 cup plain Greek yogurt (or coconut yogurt for dairy-free)
- 1/2 teaspoon vanilla extract
- 1-2 packets of stevia (or to taste)
- 1 cup ice cubes (optional, for a colder smoothie)

Instructions:

1. **Blend Ingredients:**
   - In a blender, combine the sliced banana, peanut butter, almond milk, Greek yogurt, vanilla extract, and stevia.
2. **Blend Until Smooth:**
   - Blend on high speed until the mixture is smooth and creamy. If you prefer a thicker smoothie, add more ice cubes and blend again until desired consistency is reached.
3. **Taste and Adjust:**
   - Taste the smoothie and adjust sweetness by adding more stevia if desired.
4. **Serve:**
   - Pour the smoothie into glasses and serve immediately.

Tips:

- **Frozen Banana:** For a thicker and colder smoothie, you can use frozen banana slices instead of fresh. This will eliminate the need for additional ice cubes.
- **Protein Boost:** Add a scoop of vanilla or chocolate protein powder to increase the protein content of the smoothie.
- **Nut-Free Option:** If you have a nut allergy, you can substitute the peanut butter with sunflower seed butter or tahini.
- **Toppings:** Garnish your smoothie with a sprinkle of cinnamon, a drizzle of sugar-free chocolate syrup, or a few banana slices for presentation.

This Peanut Butter Banana Smoothie is creamy, satisfying, and packed with flavor. It makes for a great breakfast or post-workout snack, providing a good balance of protein, healthy fats, and carbohydrates. Enjoy!

Sugar-Free Lemon Coconut Macaroons

Ingredients:

- 2 cups unsweetened shredded coconut
- 1/2 cup almond flour
- Zest of 1-2 lemons (depending on desired lemon flavor)
- 1/3 cup powdered erythritol (or sweetener of your choice)
- 1/4 cup melted coconut oil
- 2 large eggs
- 1 teaspoon vanilla extract
- Pinch of salt

Instructions:

1. **Preheat Oven and Prepare Baking Sheet:**
    - Preheat your oven to 325°F (160°C). Line a baking sheet with parchment paper.
2. **Mix Ingredients:**
    - In a large mixing bowl, combine the unsweetened shredded coconut, almond flour, lemon zest, powdered erythritol, melted coconut oil, eggs, vanilla extract, and a pinch of salt. Mix well until all ingredients are thoroughly combined.
3. **Form Macaroons:**
    - Take about 1 tablespoon of the mixture at a time and form it into compact balls using your hands. Place each ball onto the prepared baking sheet, spacing them about 1 inch apart.
4. **Bake:**
    - Bake in the preheated oven for 20-25 minutes, or until the macaroons are golden brown on the outside.
5. **Cool:**
    - Remove from the oven and let the macaroons cool on the baking sheet for about 10 minutes.
6. **Serve:**
    - Transfer the macaroons to a wire rack to cool completely before serving.

Tips:

- **Storage:** Store these Sugar-Free Lemon Coconut Macaroons in an airtight container at room temperature for up to a week. They can also be stored in the refrigerator for longer freshness.
- **Lemon Zest:** Adjust the amount of lemon zest based on your preference for a more or less pronounced lemon flavor.
- **Variations:** If you prefer a sweeter taste, you can add a few drops of liquid stevia or increase the amount of powdered erythritol.
- **Optional Drizzle:** For an extra touch, you can drizzle melted sugar-free chocolate over the cooled macaroons before serving.

These Sugar-Free Lemon Coconut Macaroons are a wonderful treat that combines the tropical taste of coconut with the refreshing zest of lemon, all without the added sugars. Enjoy these guilt-free delights!

Almond Flour Zucchini Bread

Ingredients:

- 2 cups almond flour
- 1/4 cup coconut flour
- 1 teaspoon baking powder
- 1/2 teaspoon baking soda
- 1/2 teaspoon salt
- 1 teaspoon ground cinnamon
- 1/2 teaspoon ground nutmeg (optional)
- 3 large eggs
- 1/4 cup melted coconut oil or unsalted butter
- 1/3 cup powdered erythritol (or sweetener of your choice)
- 1 teaspoon vanilla extract
- 1 1/2 cups grated zucchini (about 1 medium zucchini)
- Optional: 1/2 cup chopped nuts (such as walnuts or pecans)

Instructions:

1. **Preheat Oven and Prepare Pan:**
   - Preheat your oven to 350°F (175°C). Grease or line a 9x5-inch loaf pan with parchment paper.
2. **Mix Dry Ingredients:**
   - In a large bowl, whisk together almond flour, coconut flour, baking powder, baking soda, salt, cinnamon, and nutmeg (if using).
3. **Mix Wet Ingredients:**
   - In another bowl, whisk together eggs, melted coconut oil or butter, powdered erythritol, and vanilla extract until well combined.
4. **Combine Wet and Dry Ingredients:**
   - Pour the wet ingredients into the dry ingredients and stir until just combined.
5. **Add Zucchini (and Nuts, if using):**
   - Fold in the grated zucchini and chopped nuts (if using) until evenly distributed throughout the batter.
6. **Bake:**
   - Pour the batter into the prepared loaf pan and spread it out evenly.
7. **Bake:**

- Bake in the preheated oven for 50-60 minutes, or until a toothpick inserted into the center comes out clean.

8. **Cool:**
    - Allow the zucchini bread to cool in the pan for 10 minutes, then transfer it to a wire rack to cool completely before slicing.

9. **Serve:**
    - Slice and serve your Almond Flour Zucchini Bread plain or with a spread of butter or cream cheese.

Tips:

- **Storage:** Store any leftover zucchini bread in an airtight container at room temperature for up to 3 days, or refrigerate for longer freshness.
- **Zucchini Preparation:** When grating the zucchini, you can leave the skin on for added texture and nutrition.
- **Sweetness:** Adjust the sweetness to your preference by adding more or less powdered erythritol.
- **Variations:** For added flavor, you can stir in a handful of sugar-free chocolate chips or dried cranberries.

This Almond Flour Zucchini Bread is moist, flavorful, and packed with healthy ingredients. Enjoy it as a nutritious breakfast or snack!

Chocolate Almond Butter Cups

Ingredients:

- 1/2 cup almond butter (natural, unsweetened)
- 2 tablespoons coconut oil, melted
- 2 tablespoons powdered erythritol (or sweetener of your choice), divided
- 1/2 teaspoon vanilla extract
- 1/4 teaspoon salt
- 1 cup sugar-free chocolate chips or chopped dark chocolate
- Optional: Flaky sea salt for topping

Instructions:

1. **Prepare Muffin Tin:**
    - Line a mini muffin tin with paper or silicone liners (about 12 cavities).
2. **Make Almond Butter Filling:**
    - In a small bowl, mix together almond butter, melted coconut oil, 1 tablespoon of powdered erythritol, vanilla extract, and salt until smooth and well combined. Taste and adjust sweetness if desired.
3. **Melt Chocolate:**
    - In a microwave-safe bowl or using a double boiler, melt the sugar-free chocolate chips or chopped dark chocolate until smooth. Stir in the remaining 1 tablespoon of powdered erythritol.
4. **Assemble Almond Butter Cups:**
    - Spoon a small amount of melted chocolate into the bottom of each lined muffin tin cavity, spreading it slightly up the sides.
    - Place a small spoonful of almond butter filling on top of the chocolate layer in each cavity, pressing down slightly to flatten.
5. **Top with Chocolate:**
    - Spoon the remaining melted chocolate over the almond butter filling, covering it completely and smoothing the top with a spoon.
6. **Chill:**
    - Sprinkle with flaky sea salt if desired. Place the muffin tin in the refrigerator for about 30 minutes, or until the chocolate is set.
7. **Serve:**
    - Once set, remove the almond butter cups from the muffin tin and enjoy! Store any leftovers in an airtight container in the refrigerator.

Tips:

- **Variations:** You can use any nut butter of your choice instead of almond butter, such as peanut butter or cashew butter.
- **Storage:** Store these Chocolate Almond Butter Cups in the refrigerator for up to 2 weeks, or freeze them for longer storage.
- **Sweetness:** Adjust the sweetness by adding more or less powdered erythritol according to your taste preference.

These Chocolate Almond Butter Cups are a delicious and healthier alternative to traditional candy, perfect for a keto or low-carb diet. Enjoy these decadent treats guilt-free!

Low-Carb Pumpkin Cheesecake Bars

Ingredients:

Crust:

- 1 cup almond flour
- 1/4 cup powdered erythritol (or sweetener of your choice)
- 1/4 cup melted butter
- 1/2 teaspoon ground cinnamon

Cheesecake Filling:

- 16 oz (2 blocks) cream cheese, softened
- 1/2 cup powdered erythritol (or sweetener of your choice)
- 1 teaspoon vanilla extract
- 2 large eggs
- 1/2 cup pumpkin puree (unsweetened)
- 1 teaspoon ground cinnamon
- 1/2 teaspoon ground nutmeg
- 1/4 teaspoon ground cloves
- 1/4 teaspoon ground ginger

Instructions:

1. Preheat Oven and Prepare Pan:

- Preheat your oven to 325°F (160°C). Grease or line an 8x8 inch baking pan with parchment paper, leaving some overhang for easy removal.

2. Make the Crust:

- In a medium bowl, combine almond flour, powdered erythritol, melted butter, and ground cinnamon. Mix until well combined and crumbly. Press the mixture evenly into the bottom of the prepared baking pan.

3. Bake the Crust:

- Bake the crust in the preheated oven for 10 minutes. Remove from the oven and let it cool slightly while preparing the filling.

4. Prepare the Cheesecake Filling:

- In a large mixing bowl, beat the softened cream cheese until smooth and creamy.
- Add powdered erythritol and vanilla extract, and beat until well combined.
- Add eggs, one at a time, mixing well after each addition.
- Add pumpkin puree, ground cinnamon, nutmeg, cloves, and ginger. Mix until smooth and creamy.

5. Assemble and Bake:

- Pour the cheesecake filling over the baked crust, spreading it out evenly with a spatula.

6. Bake the Cheesecake Bars:

- Bake in the preheated oven for 30-35 minutes, or until the edges are set and the center is slightly jiggly.

7. Cool and Chill:

- Remove from the oven and let the cheesecake bars cool in the pan for 1 hour. Then, transfer to the refrigerator and chill for at least 2 hours, or until completely set.

8. Serve:

- Once chilled and set, lift the cheesecake bars out of the pan using the parchment paper overhang. Cut into squares and serve.

Tips:

- **Storage:** Store any leftover cheesecake bars in an airtight container in the refrigerator for up to 5 days.
- **Sweetness:** Adjust the sweetness to your taste by adding more or less powdered erythritol.
- **Crust Variation:** For a nut-free option, you can use crushed sugar-free graham crackers or coconut flour for the crust.

These Low-Carb Pumpkin Cheesecake Bars are creamy, flavorful, and perfect for satisfying your pumpkin spice cravings without the guilt. Enjoy them as a delicious dessert or treat for any occasion!

Sugar-Free Cinnamon Apple Crisp

Ingredients:

For the Apple Filling:

- 4-5 medium apples (such as Granny Smith or Honeycrisp), peeled, cored, and thinly sliced
- 2 tablespoons lemon juice
- 1/4 cup powdered erythritol (or sweetener of your choice)
- 1 teaspoon ground cinnamon
- 1/4 teaspoon ground nutmeg
- 1/4 teaspoon ground cloves
- 1 tablespoon arrowroot powder (or cornstarch, to thicken)

For the Crisp Topping:

- 1 cup almond flour
- 1/2 cup chopped pecans or walnuts
- 1/4 cup shredded unsweetened coconut
- 1/4 cup powdered erythritol (or sweetener of your choice)
- 1 teaspoon ground cinnamon
- 1/4 teaspoon salt
- 1/4 cup melted butter or coconut oil
- Optional: Sugar-free vanilla ice cream or whipped cream for serving

Instructions:

1. Preheat Oven:

- Preheat your oven to 350°F (175°C). Grease or lightly oil an 8x8 inch baking dish.

2. Prepare the Apple Filling:

- In a large bowl, toss the sliced apples with lemon juice to prevent browning.
- Add powdered erythritol, ground cinnamon, nutmeg, cloves, and arrowroot powder. Stir until the apples are evenly coated.

3. Make the Crisp Topping:

- In another bowl, combine almond flour, chopped pecans or walnuts, shredded coconut, powdered erythritol, ground cinnamon, and salt.

- Pour melted butter or coconut oil over the dry ingredients and mix until crumbly and well combined.

4. Assemble and Bake:

- Spread the apple mixture evenly in the prepared baking dish.
- Sprinkle the crisp topping evenly over the apples, covering them completely.

5. Bake the Crisp:

- Bake in the preheated oven for 35-40 minutes, or until the topping is golden brown and the apples are tender.

6. Serve:

- Remove from the oven and let cool slightly before serving.
- Serve warm, optionally topped with sugar-free vanilla ice cream or whipped cream.

Tips:

- **Apples:** Use apples that hold their shape well when baked, such as Granny Smith or Honeycrisp. Adjust sweetness based on the tartness of the apples.
- **Storage:** Store any leftover cinnamon apple crisp in the refrigerator for up to 3 days. Reheat before serving.
- **Variations:** Feel free to add a handful of sugar-free chocolate chips or raisins to the apple filling for added flavor.

This Sugar-Free Cinnamon Apple Crisp is a comforting and wholesome dessert that's perfect for any occasion. Enjoy the warm, cinnamon-spiced apples and crunchy topping guilt-free!

Blueberry Coconut Flour Muffins

Ingredients:

- 1/2 cup coconut flour
- 1/4 cup powdered erythritol (or sweetener of your choice)
- 1 teaspoon baking powder
- 1/4 teaspoon salt
- 4 large eggs
- 1/2 cup coconut oil, melted
- 1/2 cup unsweetened almond milk (or any milk of your choice)
- 1 teaspoon vanilla extract
- 1 cup fresh or frozen blueberries

Instructions:

1. **Preheat Oven and Prepare Muffin Pan:**
   - Preheat your oven to 350°F (175°C). Line a muffin tin with paper liners or grease each cavity with coconut oil.
2. **Mix Dry Ingredients:**
   - In a medium bowl, whisk together coconut flour, powdered erythritol, baking powder, and salt until well combined. Break up any clumps in the coconut flour.
3. **Combine Wet Ingredients:**
   - In another bowl, whisk together eggs, melted coconut oil, almond milk, and vanilla extract until smooth.
4. **Combine Wet and Dry Ingredients:**
   - Pour the wet ingredients into the bowl of dry ingredients. Stir until just combined and there are no dry patches of flour.
5. **Fold in Blueberries:**
   - Gently fold in the blueberries until evenly distributed throughout the batter. Be careful not to overmix to avoid crushing the blueberries.
6. **Fill Muffin Pan:**
   - Spoon the batter evenly into the prepared muffin tin, filling each cavity about 3/4 full.
7. **Bake:**
   - Bake in the preheated oven for 20-25 minutes, or until the tops are golden brown and a toothpick inserted into the center comes out clean.
8. **Cool and Serve:**

- Remove the muffins from the oven and let them cool in the pan for 5 minutes. Then transfer them to a wire rack to cool completely.

Tips:

- **Storage:** Store any leftover muffins in an airtight container at room temperature for up to 3 days, or refrigerate for longer freshness.
- **Blueberries:** If using frozen blueberries, do not thaw them before folding into the batter to prevent excess moisture.
- **Variations:** You can add a tablespoon of lemon zest for a lemon-blueberry flavor twist or sprinkle the tops with a little extra erythritol for a sweeter finish.

These Blueberry Coconut Flour Muffins are moist, fluffy, and bursting with juicy blueberries. They make for a satisfying breakfast or a wholesome snack any time of the day!

Avocado Lime Ice Cream

Ingredients:

- 2 ripe avocados
- 1/2 cup full-fat coconut milk (from a can)
- 1/4 cup powdered erythritol (or sweetener of your choice), adjust to taste
- Zest and juice of 2 limes
- 1 teaspoon vanilla extract
- Pinch of salt

Instructions:

1. **Prepare Avocados:**
   - Cut the avocados in half, remove the pits, and scoop the flesh into a blender or food processor.
2. **Blend Ingredients:**
   - Add coconut milk, powdered erythritol, lime zest, lime juice, vanilla extract, and a pinch of salt to the blender with the avocados.
3. **Blend Until Smooth:**
   - Blend until the mixture is smooth and creamy, scraping down the sides of the blender or food processor as needed.
4. **Taste and Adjust:**
   - Taste the mixture and adjust sweetness and lime flavor by adding more powdered erythritol or lime juice/zest as desired.
5. **Chill:**
   - Transfer the ice cream mixture to a bowl or container and refrigerate for at least 1-2 hours, or until thoroughly chilled.
6. **Churn in Ice Cream Maker (Optional):**
   - If you have an ice cream maker, churn the mixture according to the manufacturer's instructions until it reaches a soft-serve consistency.
7. **Freeze:**
   - If you don't have an ice cream maker, pour the chilled mixture into a freezer-safe container. Place it in the freezer and stir every 30 minutes for the first 2-3 hours to break up ice crystals and achieve a creamy texture.
8. **Serve:**
   - Once the avocado lime ice cream reaches the desired consistency, scoop it into bowls or cones and enjoy immediately.

Tips:

- **Ripe Avocados:** Make sure your avocados are ripe and creamy for the best texture.
- **Storage:** Store any leftover ice cream in an airtight container in the freezer. Let it sit at room temperature for a few minutes before scooping.
- **Variations:** For added texture and flavor, you can fold in chopped nuts or swirl in sugar-free chocolate chunks before freezing.

This Avocado Lime Ice Cream is a delightful and healthy dessert option, packed with good fats from avocados and refreshing citrus flavors from lime. Enjoy this creamy treat guilt-free!

www.ingramcontent.com/pod-product-compliance
Lightning Source LLC
LaVergne TN
LVHW081612060526
838201LV00054B/2220